The Bitter Harvest

Tony Ralls

New Wine Press

New Wine Press
P.O. Box 17
Chichester
West Sussex PO20 6RY

ISBN 0 947852 25 5

Dedication

To Linda my wife and Abigail and Naomi my children who are a constant support to me in the ministry that God has called me to. And also to all who are praying for, and seeking to reach out to those in the various problem areas of our societies with the practical love of Jesus.

About the Author

Michael Tony Ralls was born December 24th 1944. After a disturbed childhood he was constantly in trouble with the Police which resulted in him ending up with twenty two criminal convictions and for some years he was a drug addict in the West End of London in the Sixties.

Tony has been off drugs for over fifteen years; he is married to Linda who is a psychology student at Exeter University, and has two children, Abigail and Naomi. His greatest wish is that this book will help you to have a better understanding of how certain social problems have come about and also that it may leave you better equipped to deal with people who are the casualties of the various messages of the Sixties.

Tony is involved in the leadership of the YMCA in Sidmouth, Devon, England, and is a full time worker with Prison Fellowship, a charity working with prisons and Youth Custody Centres. Part of his role is to train people to be better equipped to help those in trouble and with his wife Linda he ran a house for three years where many in need came for help.

He is in constant contact with various special-needs situations and travels widely in his work to educate the public concerning social problems and Christ's answers. He often speaks at schools, Rotaries, Churches, Prisons, and has taken part in many radio and TV programmes.

He is the author of 'Escape to Reality', his autobiography and co-author of 'Snatched from the Flames', the autobiography of Anita, who was a registered drug addict for seventeen years. He is also the author of the book 'What everyone should know about drugs' and often shares with Church leaders concerning the social problems and how to respond to them practically.

Acknowledgements

This book is a product of a team effort. I would like to thank Jean Allsup for her constant patience as she re-typed manuscripts and generally encouraged me. Also the constant support of Dave Allsup and other Trustees of Stepping Stones Fellowship Trust, Devon; and the Trustees, staff and members of Prison Fellowship for their encouragement and support. I would also like to acknowledge the help of Jason Richards who at the moment resides in Gartree Prison, for his constant encouragement and practical help. Last, but not least, Ed Harding for his guidance, expertise and patience.

Michael Tony Ralls 1987

Contents

Introduction

"The thief comes only to steal and kill and destroy; I have come that they may have life, and have it to the full."

John 10:10 NIV

Psychiatrists, psychologists, welfare agencies, law enforcement agencies and politicians are all desperately seeking to find solutions to the problems that are surfacing in this day and age.

Many older people are confused and frightened at what is happening to the young, and the manifestation of evil that is being seen throughout the world.

If society rejects God and the spiritual dimension to life then the only resources that men and women have left are monetary, psychological and psychiatric. Even though these resources can sometimes be of help to the mind and soul, ultimately they can be of no help in the spiritual dimension.

If people have opened themselves up to spiritual oppression only the Spirit of God can set them free from the enemy who has bound them.

As young people grow up in the climate of permissiveness it reminds me of an illustration of the expression 'hooked', which describes the condition of a person who is addicted to drugs:

Picture a salmon swimming up the river. When it looked up it only saw the bait, it couldn't see the hook, and so it swallowed that which looked so attractive. The hook then bit deeply into its mouth. Even if that salmon is thrown back into the river and able to carry on living the marks of that hook will stay with it. Similarly many young people are being lured into ways of life which are leaving many emotional scars.

All the resources of the Western world are stretched to their limits in seeking to contain the problems that are surfacing in so many different areas. The Christian Church, empowered by, and manifesting the gifts of the Holy Spirit is the only hope that the world has got. There are times when addiction to a destructive way of life can only be helped by a supernatural healing of the Holy Spirit. However, this ministry has to be given through Christians in the context of the twentieth century and the problems that are facing mankind. I hope through this book you will find yourself better equipped to be an instrument of healing and deliverance, better able to minister in the name of Jesus, realistically counting the cost of stepping out in faith and yet reassured that Jesus will be alongside you. I also hope that you will be left with a better understanding of the pressures facing the young of today. I have heard it said that 'young people have never had it so good'. I disagree. I believe they have never had it so bad. The pressures on them are tremendous, the temptations varied, and they need our understanding and help. I believe that all social problems have spiritual roots and therefore need spiritual answers.

Michael Tony Ralls, Summer 1987

CHAPTER 1

The Seeds Sown

"They sow the wind and reap the whirlwind"
Hosea 8:7 NIV

"As I have observed, those who plough evil and those who sow trouble reap it".
Job 4:8 NIV

Throughout history, even before the world was created, the Bible tells us spiritual warfare was being waged, God with his angels on onc sidc, Satan with his fallen angels (demons) on the other. The place this warfare has been waged has been both in the heavenly realms but also here on earth, the ultimate battle being in and for the hearts and minds of those that God loves so much — mankind. The Bible also tells us that God so loved the world that He sent His only son to express His love upon the cross and to provide the way into a living relationship with a loving God (John 3:16). Jesus not only provided this way for the world but He also exposed the realm of Satan. Jesus Himself said that He had not come to condemn the world but to save it. (John 3:17). On the one side we have God, the God of light, seeking to enlighten and save people who have been cut off from Him by wrong-doing, and on the other side we have Satan who is seeking to blind and deceive and lead people to eternal destruction.

In any ongoing war fresh initiatives are launched. Many people look at the Sixties and see it as a time of liberation for young people, a time when the moral restraints of the past were thrown off, a time when young people had come into their own. It may have been right to see some of the Victorian principles as hyprocritical and pharasaical, with the Church rooted in old traditions and often out of touch, but these new messages of freedom were to bring far more bondage and hurt. One of the most destructive messages was permissiveness, no need for moral restraint. Sexual liberation was in, marriage was out, the young were at last free. The effects of permissiveness on today's society are horrendous; in 1984 in Great Britain 4,278 mothers were aged under sixteen and a further 8,842 were aged sixteen. Added to that there were 9,600 conceptions to under sixteens, fifty-six per cent of these leading to abortions forty-four per cent leading to births. For under twenties there were 118,200 conceptions, sixty-seven per cent leading to births and thirty-three per cent leading to abortions. It is perhaps easy to understand why there have now been over three million abortions since 1967. The spiritual implications of these figures are horrific. It would be easy to condemn the people who have the abortions and their acts and yet there must be a corporate responsibility also for this state of affairs. The divorce rate remains high and the implications of this are often seen in rising young offender rates and the whole stability of society is undermined. Sexual abuse and violence towards children within homes shows us this, coupled with the fact that in a society of 60,000,000, over 150,000 children are in care for a variety of reasons. Human respect for life has dropped below animals, as they at least look after their young until they are ready to fend for themselves.

The pornography industry continues to grow and whereas horror is expressed quite rightly at sexual offences against children, society does not seem to understand that if you pour enough poison into a body it will eventually be affected. We have seen how much poison has been poured into the minds of many throughout the years, through all aspects of the media. There are even pressure groups for legalising sex with children and homosexuality is more actively being promoted as normal and acceptable in society.

It is therefore not surprising to find that sixty per cent of people in our prisons are under twenty-five and that many are from broken homes. It is still the exception rather than the rule that a person from a good, stable home ends up in trouble with the law.

Sexual disease is rearing its ugly head; alongside the better known sexually transmitted diseases we now have AIDS. The emotional, spiritual and practical consequences of this message are indeed horrendous.

Some play with ouija, and even though there is always some lasting damage caused through such experience, some do make it seem that they are able to cope with it. Others dabble with other occult experiences, whether they be séances done as a sort of party game, reading the stars, or dabbling with any other aspects of the occult that comes across their path, thus sometimes leading to a direct Satanic experience. Some dip into Eastern religions which were of course so popular in the Sixties. Again, some pass on from this, but others get sucked into the religious whirlpool and so end up confused and when they meet the truth of God embodied in Jesus are unable to comprehend what it is all about.

It has been proved that childhood experiences affect the way that we are. Psychologists and psychiatrists acknowledge that the first few years of our lives are the formative years and it is during those years that life-time habits and patterns can be formed in our personalities. It has also been suggested that the foetus in the womb can be affected. Spiritually we are the same. I believe that all bad experiences and all dabbling ultimately have some sort of spiritual effect upon individual lives and wider implications in society.

We had the psychedelic era, many colours, outlandish music. Carnaby Street thrived and became the centre of fashion. The backcloth to much of this was LSD. Again, many came through this era, but many were not so fortunate. Some ended up vegetables through bad drug trips and many either died or were never the same again after a trip went wrong.

Yes, Satan planned the strategy, and he made a successful job of it. The deceived were leading the deceived. God was being rejected and though the problem of drugs was still small in comparison with the numbers of young people not taking drugs, the tiniest spot of cancer had embedded itself in Western societies and this cancer would slowly but surely spread.

Today we live with the fruit of those messages. The

seeds were sown then but we are reaping a very bitter harvest today, twenty or so years later. Books on the occult are widely read, astrology is becoming so popular that TV stations now have their own astrologers who they promote. Hardly any paper today does not carry a column of astrology and many people read to find out what their stars say. In penal institutions I go to, many times we have to pray for people to be set free from occult experiences.

Pop Festivals were becoming popular, perhaps the most famous of all of them at the time being Woodstock. Peace and love was the message. Make love not war was the idealistic message at that time. In the background yet again was music, drugs, sex and the so called message of freedom. The disciples were being trained. They were learning to worship, not the living God, but mortal creatures made of flesh and blood. We read of orgies and sacrifices in the Old Testament. It was an old message from the dark ages wrapped up to be made attractive to the modern generation.

Some professors on the campuses of America proclaimed another message, namely, that through drugs, particularly LSD and marajuana, one could find this inner awareness, a spirituality, an insight into another world. This mixed with the 'God is dead' message, plus permissiveness — do what you like — be free of all moral restraints, sounded very attractive to young people, but it was an explosive cocktail which was to blow up in the faces of a lot of misled young people. How right the Bible is when describing false teachers and prophets and also their messages. *'They promise them freedom, while they themselves are slaves of depravity'.* 2 Peter 2:19 NIV

Some might still remember the San Fransisco scene. Young people disillusioned with materialism and disappointed with life, listened to the message of freedom and flocked in their thousands to San Fransisco. Here many smoked 'pot' and grew their hair long, openly rebelling against all authority in a peaceful way. Many thought it was a phase that would pass. To an extent they were right, but seeds were being sown. Other nations followed in the footsteps of what was happening in America. It is important to understand the implications of the messages of the Sixties as permissiveness, the occult, drugs and Eastern religion were all offered as alternative ways of life. We now realise perhaps that these messages were seeds sown into the body and mind of society and they are reaping a bitter harvest today. The messages were being brought to the younger generation through the one medium guaranteed to make contact with all young people — music.

CHAPTER 2

The Messengers

The wrath of God is being revealed from heaven against all the godlessness and wickedness of men who suppress the truth by their wickedness, since what may be known about God is plain to them, because God has made it plain to them, For since the creation of the world God's invisible qualities — his eternal power and divine nature — have been clearly seen, being understood from what has been made, so that men are without any excuse.

For although they knew God, they neither glorified him as God nor gave thanks to him, but their thinking became futile and their foolish hearts were darkened. Although they claimed to be wise, they became fools and exchanged the glory of the immortal God for images made to look like mortal man and birds and animals and reptiles.

Therefore God gave them over in the sinful desires of their hearts to sexual impurity for the degrading of their bodies with one another. They exchanged the truth of God for a lie, and worshipped and served created things rather than the Creator — who is forever praised. Amen. Romans 1:18—25 NIV

Music has always been a very powerful influence. All civilizations have their own music with which they identify. Many in history marched to war accompanied by martial music and despite the fact that there may be many elements of the pop music today which do have a bad influence upon people, there are also some forms of classical music which are not spiritually healthy either.

Music can affect the mood of an individual. So it is important to have some understanding of the implications of the music of the Sixties.

It is generally recognised by many that the Sixties were the explosion point where many new groups and sounds rocketed to the attention of the public. Elvis Presley was probably the first singer who attracted the attention of the younger generation. Those who were promotionally minded and involved in the marketing of this industry realised the potential there was through music.

Suddenly many new groups shot to fame. Often young boys in their late teens or perhaps early twenties came from the position of being on the dole queue or in very ordinary work to suddenly being the focal point of the media and screaming hordes of young people. Whereas in the past the majority of the record buying public would have been older people, suddenly it was the young people who were buying the records.

It would be easy for the Christian to condemn this as the tendency has always been for us to be legalistic and sweeping in the comments that we make, particularly concerning the pop world. Sometimes this can do a disservice to the cause of Christ as it is important for all Christians to have an understanding of what has happened in the pop world and what is currently happening.

The Beatles were the focus of much of the music of the Sixties. There is a great difference between those who write both their own music and words and those who perform the songs of other people. The professionals can sing any song that is given to them, with enough practice and if they have the right vocal range and presentation, whereas those who write their own music write from their own personal experience and observations of life, and so the phases they are going through can be communicated through the words and music they create. This can be seen very much with the Beatles particularly in the early days when there was a sort of innocence about their music which slowly and subtly changed as time passed by.

The Bible talks of having no idols before us, yet the term pop 'idol' or star has become a well-known phrase. Some groups and individual singers unknowingly, others knowingly, became the Devil's evangelists as the message of drugs, permissiveness, the occult and Eastern religion was promoted through both the lifestyles and music of the groups. This impressed itself upon the minds of thousands of young people who believed and copied those lifestyles and suffered as a result.

The Beatles and other groups went through their Eastern religion phase. Some flew out to India to sit under the feet of gurus, but when they wanted to they were able to fly back home with first class plane tickets. Countless youngsters from Western nations followed them out, but not all were able to get back. Some died, some are still out there and many did not find the enlightenment that they thought they would.

As every individual has taste preferences for food so it is with music. There were all sorts of little sub-cultures within the music culture who would listen to certain types of music, and particularly in the Sixties there were those who could be identified by the music they listened to.

In recent years a film was made called 'Quadraphenia'. This was the story of a mod who took pills and was mad on scooters. He worked in a city, went to parties and now and then at weekends would go down to the coast for a bit of fun, whether it be rioting or picking up girls. In the end he committed suicide by going over a cliff. The backcloth to this film was music and the story showed a person who could not separate fantasy from reality. How true this was for so many. I am the first to agree that not all mods were into pills and taking 'speed' as it was known, but many did and they also had the music they identified with and the lifestyle that went with it. Of course not everyone died and many did grow through this phase, but many did not.

The Rolling Stones were another group who were very popular. One L.P. which became very famous was 'His Satanic Majesty'. In those days certain elements of the occult were promoted through music, and today there are still those groups that are well-known for using occult imagery in promoting their music.

I pray with many lads in Youth Custody Centres who have to be set free from occult experiences. One particular lad who I was chatting to after prayer shared with me that even though he was a Christian and loved Jesus he still found anti-Christ type words coming to his lips. These had been imbibed by him through listening to songs and music which were of an anti-Christ nature. So even as a Christian he found great difficulty in putting this aside.

Brian Jones of the Rolling Stones was to die, one of many drug-related deaths. It is generally recognised that many groups in those days were experimenting with various forms of drugs and hence the music was contaminated through this experimentation.

In America we had the San Francisco scene which I have already touched upon. A very popular record in those days was by the Flower People with the words: "Have you been to San Francisco? Have you worn flowers in your hair?" To us many years later these words seem trite and trivial, and yet at that time it touched a chord in the hearts of young people who were open to these messages. There were those who listened to softer music which was more associated with LSD and with smoking marajuana.

Bob Marley rose to fame later with his many L.P.s rooted in Rastafarianism which promoted promiscuousness and also the smoking of ganja which is another word for marajuana.

So there were different cultures of young people who were listening to different forms of music. Even though every young person who was into pop music in those days was most definitely not into drugs, or necessarily into permissiveness, the messages slowly but surely were passed into the minds of all young people in the western civilizations through the radio and TV stations around the world.

If I was the Devil and had a message which I wished to communicate to young people, music would be the medium through which I would do it. I believe that the Devil did have a message which sounded very attractive to young people, so he communicated it through instruments willing to be used even if perhaps sometimes unknowingly. The seeds were being sown and continue to be sown in the minds of countless thousands of young people.

The drug abuse in our world has now grown to tremendous proportions. In the Sixties there was always the backcloth of music to which drug taking went on. Perhaps things have changed but I still believe that there is a direct link between music and the problems that there are amongst young people today.

Many who would refuse to worship God nevertheless accept worshipping Man as a substitute and so live with the consequences. I fervently believe in the second coming of Jesus Christ and that many of the signs indicating that He could come quite soon are already in the world.

I believe that there will also be an Anti-Christ, and that what has happened with young people over the last twenty years or so is part of the preparation of the coming of the Anti-Christ, who is probably alive today.

John the Baptist came to prepare the way for Jesus. He who came from the highest place came humbly to this earth to proclaim salvation. He that is coming from the lowest part of the earth will also demand worship and respect. Music has played its part and is playing its part in preparing people for the worship of such a man. A time of preparation is going on to set the stage in the world for the coming of the Anti-Christ who will be the Devil in the flesh.

Many pop stars were to die — Jimmy Hendrix, Janis Joplin, Keith Moon, Brian Jones of the Rolling Stones and countless others either through drug overdoses or drug-related deaths. These deaths hit the headlines, not so the many deaths of young people who died in toilets, parks or dirty bed-sits. They did not warrant headlines. They had indeed been led astray, many unable to live up to the demands of the lifestyles that were being portrayed by those they looked to.

Many actresses and actors also had drug problems that needed to be treated. To be on drugs was to be 'in'. I remember the Sixties so well — the feeling of exaltation. We had found freedom, or so we thought. I know that not everyone was sleeping around, and not everyone was taking drugs, but I do believe that a spot of cancer had been planted within society. As with cancer which quite often is not discovered until too late so we are now discovering the social and spiritual consequences of the messages that were being planted within society in the Sixties.

As time has passed so the media has been affected by all the messages. Children's programmes can even have occult symbolism. Many occult films have been produced over the years because much money can be made through producing these films. Also plays on television and films have become more sexually explicit as time has passed. Actors and actresses pre-1960 would have hidden the fact that they were getting a divorce, but now it is the exception rather than the rule where partners stay together in the film industry. So slowly but surely the whole of the media has been affected.

The Sixties were a pivotal time. We have certainly moved on into something new, but I think the implications of what we as society have moved into are horrendous.

We read in the Bible of false prophets and teachers and perhaps in our minds we have the general idea of people with long white hair, beards and perhaps robes, and have not been able to see that a false prophet doesn't necessarily have to be old. A false prophet doesn't necessarily have to know he is being used directly by Satan. One of the titles of Satan is the Deceiver. There are many deceived people who are deceiving others without fully realising the implications of both their action and their words. It must be recognised that if we buy an L.P., go to see a film, or contribute to any literature which is damaging we are supporting the work that is being done. Christians recognise this in that they support those who they feel are doing good works for God, and so it works the other way.

It is important that we assess what we spend our money on, particularly when it comes to music, videos and going to see films.

Today much is changing. We have those who are openly homosexual or bi-sexual who are becoming the heroes of the young. We have had the punk era with the anti-hero phase. In certain films we have the vigilante hero who through force and violence deals with the evil in the world. In fact we have many things which have been turned upside down.

The strength, compassion, love and enlightenment

which is our due through a personal experience with Jesus is something which many reject, and yet seek a conterfeit in other avenues of life. To be spiritually blind is not only to deny the existence of God but also the existence of Satan. Many who have come into prominence in all aspects of communication have no knowledge of God or Satan and have been used as instruments to communicate the destructive messages.

The Sixties were a time of spiritual seeking but in every other direction except God. An illustration I often use in the work I do amongst those in need is of a time when I was an addict in the West End of London. As it was raining, and as I had some money on me I decided to go to the cinema. It looked very nice from the outside and as I walked in there was thick carpet on the floor. It was very luxurious and warm. I bought my ticket and went into the cinema itself and sat in the comfortable seat and relaxed and watched the film. The film was over. I then went towards the exit and as I pushed the doors open I found myself in a back alley stinking of urine and vomit. It was one of those places which people used as a toilet if they could not make it to the public lavatories. It was just off the bright lights of Leicester Square and illustrates something of what life can be for many who are caught up in the traps. When offered the first drugs it is often in an environment that is warm and colourful. If you end up with a drugs problem you end up in that back alley often on your own.

As it is with drugs so it can be with permissiveness, drink, occult and other damaging experiences. I have found with Youth Custody lads that quite often they will commit a crime when they are with other people, but in the end they do their time on their own.

As a person who has sat through the night with those who have had abortions, and even though the physical scars have healed the emotional scars are still sore and open, as a person who has helped people to come to terms with their drug problems and to slowly but painfully build a new life, as a person who has spent much time talking to those from care backgrounds who are expressing through violence their hatred of their father or of whoever it is they feel has hurt them or rejected them I begin to realise the terrible damage that has been brought through the messages of freedom.

It was recently that I saw a TV programme which interviewed some personalities who had made their fame and fortune in the Sixties. The Sixties they talked about were not the Sixties I knew, as most of my friends died on drugs or ended up vegetables through taking LSD. There were indeed those who became rich and famous, but perhaps they never realised what was happening to many.

I have heard the term "The Swinging Sixties" and I think of it more in the terms of a hangman's noose than any implication that it was fun and great.

Music always has and always will play an important part in the lives of people. It is the backcloth against which the various messages are painted.

Young people had suddenly become a commercial market. Music is an industry as is drugs, pornography and the occult. Many millions are made out of young people. They are the future generation so ideas and thoughts implanted can continue on to the next generation. There are many who are in a God-like position in young people's lives and it is an awesome thought that those who have been worshipped by millions whether it be from the world of films, TV or music will one day stand before the throne of God. They will be called to account for what they have or haven't done with their gifts and the example set. We must pray that they realise their need of God and realise the awesome responsibility that they carry for their actions. *'If anyone causes one of these little ones who believe in me to sin it is better for him to have a large millstone hung around his neck and to be drowned in the depths of the sea. Woe to the world because of the things that cause people to sin'. Such things must come, but woe to the man through whom they come!*(Matthew 18:6—7NIV)

This scripture applies also to teachers, social workers, parents, and any who abuse their positions and cause young people to stumble.

CHAPTER 3

The Wisdom of Man

For the message of the cross is foolishness to those who are perishing, but to us who are being saved it is the power of God. For it is written:

"I will destroy the wisdom of the wise; the intelligence of the intelligent I will frustrate."

Where is the wise man? Where is the scholar? Where is the philosopher of this age? Has not God made foolish the wisdom of the world? For since in the wisdom of God the world through its wisdom did not know him, God was pleased through the foolishness of what was preached to save those who believe.

1 Corinthians 1:18—21 NIV

Do not deceive yourselves. If any one of you thinks he is wise by the standards of this age, he should become a 'fool' so that he may become wise.

For the wisdom of this world is foolishness in God's sight.

As it is written: "He catches the wise in their craftiness", and again, "the Lord knows that the thoughts of the wise are futile".

So then, no more boasting about men! All things are yours. 1 Corinthians 3:18—21 NIV

Alongside the many other messages of the Sixties was the subtle message of 'God is dead — if He was ever alive'. Academically we had outgrown the concept of God as we no longer needed to believe in something. It is interesting to note that with this message of the lack of need for a spiritual dimension came many social problems. As God's law was ignored and a new rule book on morality written, so one profession gained prominence. Psychiatrists were turned to, and so, instead of approaching the God of the Bible people now went to a variety of people to whom they confessed their sins and who in turn charged money and often treated them with drugs. Drug companies responded and suddenly there were many different forms of tranquilisers and sedatives available on the market used to treat people. Psychologists and others were only later drawn into the field of responding to the many social problems that were manifesting themselves. Although drugs can sometimes help a person they cannot ultimately cure spiritual problems with a spiritual root.

Our mental hospitals and prisons are overflowing, and yet mankind refuses to acknowledge the consequences of his actions in seeking to be God instead of submitting to God. When will people realise that if you throw away the rule book then chaos will ensue? If we ignored our traffic laws there would be chaos and killing on the roads. If we ignored the natural laws and jumped from a high building we would be badly hurt or killed. Yet Man continues to ignore God's laws and is surprised at the result.

It is important also to understand the political thinking that was going on in those days. Harold Wilson was the Prime Minister and Roy Jenkins the Home Secretary. Government by consensus was the order of the day. Again, we do not learn from what has happened in the past. Rome and many other civilizations fell to pieces when those who were supposed to lead started to entertain the masses. In Rome's days they had the Colliseum where Christians were burned, where gladiators fought lions and where blood was spilled. Today, we have our television screens and films. Immorality and the breakdown of marriage was very much the order of the day in the last days of Rome. I have often heard the expression 'we have an enemy within', but the enemy within is not only the political activist, but also a spiritual enemy, Satan.

In the Sixties parents were horrified to see pictures of Pop Festivals where people were openly having intercourse (I resist the term 'make love' as intercourse in this way has nothing to do with real love). The message was 'Make love not war'. Protests went on against the Vietnam War and all war, and it sounded very good. The Bible talks of people saying 'peace, peace, when there is no peace' and in many ways this was the Sixties.

In a physical war it is easy to see the damage and the hurt through maimed limbs, bombed cities and devastation. In the spiritual war it is less easy to see the hurts and the brokenness that has gone on in the hearts and minds of people.

I am sure that the Africans who were first approached by the white man who talked to them about religion and civilization would have been quite shocked to see some of the pictures of the Pop Festivals where young people were openly and blatently having sexual intercourse. They would have been quite fascinated to see young people jerking and dancing to the music in much the same was as they have always done. It would have amused them, I am sure, to hear them say that this is new, this is freedom.

Society began to lose its way and somehow not realise the implications of what was happening to it. We have a system of justice where a white-coated doctor who is well paid, can on demand, do an abortion on a perfectly healthy young girl with a perfectly healthy young baby and be well respected within society, yet a child from a care background can be given a youth custody centre sentence for stealing a minimal amount of money.

This message of the Sixties affected not only the young of our countries but the old as well. There were and still are many irresponsible adults who get divorced and re-married, and who is to judge the amount of damage that his sort of behaviour can do measured against a bullet which can quickly take someone's life? The psychological and emotional damage that occurs within the hearts and minds of young people through their parents being divorced cannot be nullified by a few exceptional cases where children have apparently quite healthily survived these experiences.

In my work in youth custody centres I find that there is almost a direct link between youngsters first getting into trouble and first having epileptic fits through some emotional trauma that has happened, often through the divorce of their parents.

Man was made by God in His image and likeness.

God made Man to have fellowship with Him. All have a built-in need for God. As a result of Adam and Eve choosing knowledge rather than obedience to God, we have inherited a sinful nature which gives us an unholy and unnatural rebellion against God's laws. Yet deep down there is a yearning for God, for we were made to worship Him.

Satan in his great design upon men seeks to get men to worship himself by playing upon Man's ignorance and sin to lead him astray. Satan uses the fleshly attraction to get through to soul, mind, will, emotions and intellect, to wear down the will of a person to form a physical dependency or a psychological one, to bring the will into a state of total passivity so that he can move in on the person's fallen spirit to destroy it. Wisdom is promised, but there is always a price to be paid.

In the Sixties the Welfare State had been going for some while. The Utopia which had been promised did not come about. Many expected the State to be God, able to meet all the needs in Great Britain, but of course it couldn't. Certainly there are some advantages to the Welfare State, but all the resources of the State can only minister to the body and soul of individuals and cannot touch the spirit. The main cause of the problems that are manifesting themselves in our society and in many Western societies is that society as a whole has turned its back on God.

An illustration that I have often used is a picture that I felt God gave me. It is of a very large spider's web. In the corner was a large evil-looking spider which represented the Devil. In my mind I could see all sorts of symbols which represent those things which people are attracted to; money, sex, drugs, drink, and music. Flies got to coming into close contact with the web and here and there one would actually touch the web and become entangled. The spider would then scurry out and slowly but surely bind up the fly. These flies were then left alive and yet bound up. This brought to mind something that Jesus once said about people being alive and yet dead. It also brought to mind a scripture concerning the Devil where it talks about him prowling like a roaring lion looking for someone to devour.

In many ways the spider's web illustration shows what happens to many young people today as they step out in life. Whether they become involved in drugs, permissiveness or the occult, they can certainly end up entangled and bound up.

C.S. Lewis wrote of the God-shaped hole that is within people, and I believe that addiction to a life-style that is damaging has something to do with people putting something else in that God-shaped hole. Our ears and our eyes are the inroads into our subconscious and therefore what we read or look at, what we hear, what we do with our bodies have physical, emotional and spiritual consequences. As the law continues to facilitate sin rather than seeking to curb it we have to live with the consequences. We will reap what we sow. As God is rejected so other gods will become the centre of people's lives. If we reject God then Satan has an open door to individuals. Our nations are living ruled by 'wise' men of the twentieth century who have become foolish in their wisdom. Despite forty years peace in Europe no-one can honestly say we are better off morally and spiritually.

It would be very easy to condemn those like Roy Jenkins who introduced the Homosexuality Bill, and David Steel the Leader of the Liberal Party who introduced the Abortion Act. I believe that they did not consciously do anything that they considered wrong, but were motivated by the humanistic attitudes of the day to try and right what they considered wrong in a free society.

We realise now the implications of both those bits of legislation which passed through Parliament, and the law which intended to do away with the backstreet abortionists ended up facilitating over one hundred thousand abortions a year.

The Homosexuality Bill paved the way for homosexuals to press for 'gay rights' and to pass on to young people that this way of living is normal and acceptable.

We now have legislation being approved which will do away with the term ''illegitimacy'. In essence this seems good because it means that there will be no slur on people like myself who are of illegitimate birth. It will also mean that people such as myself, if we could manage to trace our natural fathers, would be entitled to a part of the inheritance after their deaths. It will also, however, open the way for more and more people to have illegitimate children and it does not take into account the emotional damage that can be enacted in a life of rejection, hurt and lack of identity which legislation can do nothing about.

God has indeed made foolish the wisdom of the world. If we haven't learnt anything positive at all we should at least have learnt this lesson — that even if something is created for a good use Man almost certainly will find an evil use for it.

Politicians, academics, and dreamers will always come along and declare that they have the answers. Nations are becoming disillusioned, for though men promise much they deliver little.

Whether we are communists or capitalists, left or right wing in our politics, we have to come to the point where we recognise that what we sow we will reap. There are always consequences for breaking laws. If we ignore even part of the traffic laws, there still would be an increase in deaths and damage on the roads.

As Man continues to both create his own laws and ignore spiritual laws there will continue to be damage and death within our society.

Unfortunately it is usually the innocent who suffer. Once a law has been passed then it is very difficult to repeal it. The damage has been and will continue to be done long after the initiators have gone on to other things. They will have to live with their consciences and give an account to God.

CHAPTER 4

The Reaction of the Church

The word of the Lord came to me: "Son of man, speak to your countrymen and say to them: 'When I bring the sword against a land and the people of the land choose one of their men and make him their watchman, and he sees the sword coming against the land and blows the trumpet to warn the people, then if anyone hears the trumpet but does not take warning and the sword comes and takes his life, his blood will be on his own head. Since he heard the sound of the trumpet but did not take warning, his blood will be on his own head. If he had taken warning, he would have saved himself. But if the watchman sees the sword coming and does not blow the trumpet to warn the people and the sword comes and takes the life of one of them, that man will be taken away because of his sin, but I will hold the watchman accountable for his blood.'

"Son of man, I have made you a watchman for the house of Israel; so hear the word I speak and give them warning from me." Ezekiel 33:1—7 NIV

When the message of the Sixties became known in the Western civilizations, liberal theologians of some historic churches joined in and said, ''Quite right. It is O.K. to have sex outside of marriage; 'gay' is good, there is nothing wrong with it.'' Others at the opposite extreme did not condone this, but despite believing in Jesus and in the Bible withdrew from the evil world behind doctrinal statements, seeking to build a society within a society to protect both themselves and their families from the world. Now and then a doctrinal volley would be fired over the wall bringing only condemnation to many young people who were in desperate need for help. Almost as a direct result of this stand, many found that the walls which were there to protect them from the world ended up becoming prisons, and many in the Church lost contact with the very world that needed them so much. The Bible very plainly shows us that Man never changes. Despite all the advances that we have made in science, technology and the wonderful discoveries that have surfaced through the years, the heart of Man is still evil and tends more towards corruption than good. One has only got to look out on the world and see that men are like children out of contact with their father, unable to make the right decisions, unable to cope with the responsibilities that are placed upon their shoulders. In the same way that the inner nature of Man has never changed, so some aspects of the Church have not changed either. There are still the Scribes and the Pharisees. The Scribes were a group of people who could be compared to the modernists of this day. They did not believe in an afterlife, in demons or in a living contact with the living God. The Pharisees were legalists who knew their Bibles inside out, but they ruled their people with an iron rod. Legalism and tradition were very much part of their religious life. Yet despite their knowledge of Scripture they could not see in Jesus the Messiah whom God had sent. It is interesting to note that the Scribes and the Pharisees reacted in the same way to the living Saviour.

As we have looked into the problems that have surfaced through the Sixties and since, we begin to realise that we have gone in a full circle, and unless contact is made with the living God this circle will continue to go round. The watchmen were blind and did not realise their responsibilities to the world.

It is interesting to note whenever teaching is given on spiritual warfare that most emphasis is placed on Satan attacking the Christian or the body of Christ. This is of course true; Satan does attack the Christian and the Body of Christ, and yet it is not recognised that Satan is constantly also attacking the world, seeking to deceive and lead to destruction. We can see the enemy at work, and we are the ones called upon to warn, yet because of the lack of teaching on spiritual warfare and the gifts of the Holy Spirit the Church has not been equipped. The salt has stayed in its salt cellar and the world has lost its seasoning.

Two books which made a great impact were 'Honest to God' and 'The Myth of God Incarnate'. These were written by leading theologians and expressed the ideas which were in the forefront of some in the historic churches that even those who were Christians had outgrown the simplistic concepts of salvation and redemption. The fact that these books were popular shows that many indeed felt that. We are now living in the days when the Resurrection is being questioned, all aspects of the supernatural and the miraculous, and seeds are being sown to undermine the very fundamentals of Christian belief. We not only had the wise men of the world but so called 'wise men' within the Christian Church who felt they had outgrown the simplistic teaching of the Bible.

Different people have different ways of judging spirituality. For some attending church and taking the sacraments is the total fulfilment of their Christian commitment. For others attending church and going to a variety of teaching conferences is their way of life. Others have a deep knowledge of the word of God, yet I believe true spirituality can be judged through the reaction of a person who finds himself next to a promiscuous woman as Jesus did. Would you be able to relate to that woman spiritual truths and to communicate with her?

When speaking at a Carol Service at a Youth Custody Centre I became very aware of the cloak of spirituality that many western countries have got. The trappings of religion are all around us and the Church has an historic role to play in most state occasions. (2 Timothy 3:1—5). It has the form of godliness yet denies God's power.

I believe the message of the Sixties affected the Church just as much as the world. It was denuded of true spirituality and scriptures like *"The Gospel is the power of God unto salvation"* (1 Corinthians 1:18) are no longer real to many professing Christians.

Satan, I believe, succeeded not only in binding up many who are in the world and destroying many young people, but also succeeded in causing a divide between those in need and those who were the stewards of the mysteries of God.

Certain attitudes also seemed to creep into the evangelical Church concerning those who were considered the 'sinners'. The Bible has always been very clear that there were two forms of sin; the sin of commission — doing that which is wrong, and the sin of ommission — not doing that which is right. Many have concentrated on the former and not the latter. In an institution where I am a teacher there are five hundred young offenders. Over sixty percent of these are from 'care backgrounds'. In other words they are no longer in contact with their families or have come from a socially deprived background. This statistic, except for a few minor variations is the same for penal institutions in many Western nations. In Psalm 82 we see God's attitude towards law and justice, particularly in verse 3 and 4; *'Defend the cause of the weak and fatherless; maintain the rights of the poor and oppressed, rescue the weak and needy'*. It is a sad fact that those who are in the deepest need of care in our societies often receive the least amount of care and attention from the Church. I believe we are living not only with the legacy of the messages of the Sixties that came to the world but the attitudes of the Sixties which affected the Church's attitude to the world. Sometimes it would seem that the Church's role is to condemn the world, based on an in-built assumption that we are better than the sinners. 1 John 1:8—10 NIV very plainly states: *'If we claim to be without sin, we deceive ourselves and the truth is not in us. If we confess our sins He is faithful and just and will forgive us our sins and purify us from all unrighteousness.*

If we claim we have not sinned, we make him out to be a liar and His word has no place in our lives'. The sad fact has always been that we Christians sin with the knowledge of God in our lives, yet we are forgiven as we repent. We are just saved sinners reaching out to unsaved sinners.

With the breakdown in families and the many unwanted children that have been brought into this world through the permissive message it is now becoming the exception rather than the rule as to whether a child will have a good family environment. Those who have had Christian homes have a tremendous responsibility to share with others. God foreknew that I would be born illegitimate and would have a bad childhood and He has been able to turn this negative to a positive. So those who have been born into good homes, especially Christian homes, have much to offer. The Church in the Sixties failed in seeking to reach out to the casualties and this is now slowly but surely being redressed by some. The Church has to come to terms with the fact that though society classifies certain forms of sin to be worse than others, God doesn't. Sin is sin. Stealing pens from the office is as bad as committing a robbery. Whatever a person does, God always loves a sinner who comes to Him in true repentence. So when God looks down on the earth, He does not see bad people in prison and good people outside, He sees all as bad unless they have accepted Jesus as their Saviour.

So we have a two-fold message to bring to society: the good news that Jesus loves wrongdoers as people despite what they have done and that through true sorrow for sin forgiveness can be found in God. But there is also the Devil who is seeking to deceive and lead people to destruction. We come as *saved* wrongdoers to *unsaved* wrongdoers. We introduce a person who loves them, Jesus, not religion and we come with compassion, as all are like sheep who have been led astray.

Jesus was always able to draw alongside those in the world to share His message. He was known as the friend of publicans and sinners. When He met the woman at the well, a promiscuous woman with five husbands, He was able to communicate with her and had such an impact upon her that she straight away went and told others of her meeting with Him. The scriptures very plainly say that Jesus did not come to condemn the world, but to save the world. (John 3:17). It is important to note that Jesus was accepted by the publicans and sinners and rejected by the religious leaders of that day.

It would be interesting to think about what Jesus' reaction would have been to the message of the Sixties, and where one would have found Him. I feel that he would have gone amongst the young and sought to share and communicate with them.

The commission that we have as the Church is to follow the example of Jesus who left His very comfortable situation in Heaven, came and lived here on earth and died a terrible death voluntarily on our behalf.

The church I refer to of course are those who love and follow Jesus, those who are anointed by the Holy Spirit and so united in the Spirit with all who truly love and follow Jesus. This can mean people who are in historic churches or those who are in the new house churches. God, I believe, wants His people to be yoked together in the Spirit, working together as one, seeking to make contact with the lost world.

CHAPTER 5

The Move of the Spirit

"And afterward,
I will pour out my Spirit on all people.
Your sons and daughters will prophesy,
your old men will dream dreams,
Your young men will see visions.
Even on my servants, both men and women,
I will pour out my Spirit in those days."
Joel 2:28—29 NIV

In America there was a real move of the Holy Spirit in the Sixties which came to the attention of the media. Billy Graham wrote a book called the Jesus Generation. This book was about two revolutions — the 'Youth' revolution and the 'Jesus' revolution.

The 'Jesus' revolution came to the attention of such renowned publications as Time Magazine, the New York Times, the Chicago Tribune and many others. Billy Graham himself began to realise that at this time his crusades were comprised largely of youth, which was a dramatic change from the Fifties.

It was in the early Seventies that NBC produced a national television news programme on the Jesus

Movement, as did CBS. So in America there was a real move amongst young people, and although perhaps some were caught up in the emotional side of this movement many were deeply touched by the Lord during this time and went on to serve Him.

In England we did not have such a dramatic 'Jesus' revolution. I do remember being at Hyde Park with thousands upon thousands of young people for a concert which was organised by the Festival of Light. I also remember the day that Arthur Blessitt came to this country, so we did have some sort of input from America at that time.

In England the Fountain Trust movement was well known amongst those, particularly in the Anglican Church and other main line denominations, who were drawn into the Renewal Movement. I remember going to Westminster Central Hall to worship with a couple of thousand other people baptised in the Spirit.

The move of the Holy Spirit was to affect many who were part of the historic churches in Great Britain, but unfortunately it did not often spill over into the local community.

Certainly some new communities sprang up that did have a care for those who were in deep spiritual and social need. I am sure also that many individuals became more aware of the desperate needs of society as a whole. However, as is so often repeated throughout history, the mainstream of the movement of the Holy Spirit at that time got re-channelled back into seeking to renew structures within the Christian culture rather than reaching on out to society that was in such deep spiritual need.

In Genesis 11:1—9 we see a people who had refused to obey the command of God which was to go out and populate and possess the earth. In the end He sent down different languages so that they would ultimately go on to fulfil the commission that He had given them. They sought to build themselves a city and sought to make a name for themselves. They did not want to be scattered over the whole world (verse 4). So today we have many who are seeking to make a name for themselves, to build a tower unto heaven to create their own communities. As time has passed many new house church movements have come into being. God is still very much moving and seeking to bring His people to that point where they will fulfil His commission to go out into the world proclaiming the Gospel. I believe that when men seek to build a name for themselves God has to bring confusion yet again — in other words separation so that people will ultimately go out into the world and bring to it the good news that Jesus is alive.

Many perhaps did not realise that to be filled with the Holy Spirit is to be equipped to be a witness in this world. Many volunteered themselves for 'full time' Christian service, but perhaps did not realise the need for them to see society as a whole as a mission field. So few realise the need to be involved in Social Services, the Prison system, the drugs culture, the need to become Christian psychiatrists and psychologists, and so bring an element of salt to the society that is rapidly losing its seasoning.

It was during this era that many cults came into being which were to form spiritual traps for young people. The Children of God which looked so attractive to young people drew in some of those who were fed up with church orthodoxy, legalism, rituals and movements based on human traditions. Many, quite rightly, condemned the Children of God and other cults but were not willing to change in any way to offer an alternative to young people who were so desperately seeking.

Through the message of various records that were in the charts at that time and also the lifestyles of certain individuals, Eastern religions became very popular and many young people set out on this road. In England there was just as deep a hunger for spiritual things but unfortunately there was not much on offer for the young. As the years have passed I do not believe this has changed much. It is hard for Christians to accept responsibility for allowing the growth of many cults including the Jehovah's Witnesses, Christian Science, and many other new Eastern or Western religions which have captured the minds of many young or old.

There were, and still are, many within the historic churches who are responding to the move of the Spirit and I am privileged to share with many from different denominations who have stood for what God wants. One can see from what is happening in their churches that God is honouring them, and people are being saved and filled with the Holy Spirit. However, those who have made such a stand have often been through a baptism of suffering and been isolated and under much pressure because of their stand.

We have also seen a movement of the house churches

throughout the country. Some retain their liberty and are large and are ministering in a very positive way in society. Some have come under legalism and ritualism which is a far heavier bondage than many of the churches that people have come out of to join these fellowships. Even among the fellowships that are moving on with God and have resisted pressures that would seek to bring them into legalism and bondage, there is still often an inability to cope with those who come from the different sub-cultures that are in our society today.

Many emphasise the coming of Jesus and it is possible that we may be the generation that will experience this. Many hide their heads in the sand concerning the other aspects of the second coming of Jesus, i.e. that there will be an Anti-Christ, the Devil in the flesh, and that times will become harder and harder upon this earth (1 Peter 4:12—16).

I have already touched upon the false prophets and teachers who are seeking to deceive the younger generation and the fact that they have succeeded quite well over the last twenty years. However as Christians we need to be aware of the Scripture which says *"Many will come in my name, saying I am the Christ"* (Matthew 14:5 NIV). There are many who claim to be the anointed ones for this day. The claim to be a Christ is the claim to be an anointed one.

There are many who pay to go to conferences and buy teaching tapes, seeking to be better equipped to reach out into the world. They come under the feet of a diversity of different teachers yet often there seems to be no real impact upon society that they live in. I believe God's goal is that the ordinary should become extraordinary, that the ordinary member of the Body of Christ properly trained and taught and mobilised can have tremendous impact upon society. We must still look to those men who do have a message from God but we ourselves must realise the responsibility that we have for those who live around us. There is a need for many to learn to apply the truths that they receive and this means stepping out on the water like Peter did. When we are at that point of sinking we will then look up and find that Jesus will lift us up.

Some are confused after getting baptised in the Holy Spirit when times of hardship come upon them. I believe that when one is filled with the Holy Spirit one is then given the extra strength to become like Jesus in this world. We are saved through the pain of the cross. Others will be saved through the voluntary pain that we go through both emotionally, physically and spiritually as we seek to reach out to the casualties of the permissive age.

There has always been a danger that Christians would feel that being filled with the Holy Spirit is a sort of insulation against suffering in this world. Although there has been some attempt to touch the problems of those who are casualties of the permissive age, some have withdrawn very quickly when they have discovered that they have unearthed a can of worms in their midst and that helping people means to be totally involved with them. With that comes all the pressures both of satanic warfare and emotional and practical strain in seeking to help.

In the Sixties we saw, if anything, a withdrawal from

the world so that now one can go into secular situations of care and find very few Christians working. It is sad to note perhaps that many of the care institutions for children throughout the country are run by atheistic or agnostic people, and some institutions are even run by lesbians or homosexuals. It is very rare to find a Spirit-filled Christian involved in these situations and if you do find one they generally have little understanding or support from their church. I am encouraged when I do come across those who are reaching out in the name of Jesus.

As I travel to many youth custody centres, prisons and schools, I am horrified at the number of young people who have no concept of God, who have been dabbling in the occult, who are involved at early ages in permissiveness and drugs, and have already experienced sexual abuse and violence.

I believe the Church lost an opportunity in the Sixties to be an effective witness in society, and this has to change. The general attitude seems to be that if one is a Christian then everything will be all right, that to suffer emotional pain and strain is not part of the Christian's lot in this world. There has been much teaching on the Baptism in the Holy Spirit and yet little on the baptism of suffering for believers which comes as people step out in the suffering world to minister to the needs of those who have been afflicted by Satan and are emotionally damaged.

As we learn to be obedient to the call of God we will find that we come into contact with suffering and pain. We have the great example of course in Jesus our Saviour who through being obedient and suffering became the source of eternal salvation for us. (Hebrews 5:7—10). He shared in our humanity so that the power of the Devil could be broken. He became like us so that we could be saved. We have a tremendous opportunity of becoming true priests of God. Aaron was anointed with oil to be a high priest. Jesus had the dove of the Holy Spirit come upon Him at His baptism which anointed Him to be our High Priest. He set an example to us which we should follow.

The anointing and empowering of the Holy Spirit equips us to be able to stand the suffering that will come upon us as we seek to minister in the name of Jesus in this world. (Hebrews 2:14—18).

Because of the attitude towards suffering in this world there are many who would feel that they must be out of God's will or plan if they do in fact suffer. I truly believe that this world is not our home, that it is in the power of the enemy and that when we make a friend of Jesus we make an enemy of Satan. As we go through voluntary suffering in our lives, that is stepping out into areas where we don't necessarily have to go — except that the love of Christ compels us to go — then we will find a dimension in Christ which is beyond that which can be learned from Bible Studies, teaching sessions and open worship sessions. For as God comforts us in our afflictions so we will become a comfort to other people with the same comfort with which God has comforted us. (2 Corinthians 1:3—7).

CHAPTER 6

Wu Oi

"Then the King will say to those on His right, 'Come, you who are blessed by my Father; take your inheritance, the kingdom prepared for you since the creation of the world. For I was hungry and you gave me something to eat, I was thirsty and you gave me something to drink, I was a stranger and you invited me in, I needed clothes and you clothed me, I was sick and you looked after me, I was in prison and you came to visit me'.

Then the righteous will answer Him, 'Lord when did we see you hungry and feed you, or thirsty and give you something to drink?

When did we see you a stranger and invite you in, or needing clothes and clothe you? When did we see you sick or in prison and go to visit you?

The King will reply, 'I'll tell you the truth, whatever you did for one of the least of these brothers of mine, you did for me.' "

Matthew 25:34—40 NIV

Wu Oi freely translated means 'mutual love' or 'supportive love', and the Wu Oi Christian Centre in

Hong Kong provides this in abundance. As a result it has provided the salvation of countless drug abusers in Hong Kong. The Wu Oi logo displayed outside the centre symbolically indicates its major weapons in the fight against drug abuse: the Bible, the Cross and a heart, representing Christian love. The doors of the Wu Oi are always open to the drug user sincerely seeking help. Some of the men who have been helped there have been addicted to heroin for twenty or thirty years. This Christian witness in Hong Kong is much like many other Christian witnesses in other problem situations throughout the world.

I think this Chinese word sums up for us what is needed for those who are addicted to drugs and are victims of this permissive age. 'Wu Oi' says it all.

Earlier I touched on the watchman on the tower whose duty it is to warn this generation of the enemy who is coming to kill, maim and destroy. These people are like fishermen, the evangelists or 'front line troops'. The Church is often described as an army, and in an army there are different skills and abilities, companies, battalions, brigades. There are many different arms of the army which are independent and yet interdependent upon each other, and each have skills which complement each other. The infantry man in the last War needed the support of the artillery and the air force. They communicated through their radios, and so were able to indicate when they were in need of help and assistance. In the first World War listening devices were planted in the trenches which were to be occupied by the enemy. This meant that information would help the front line troops who now had some idea of what was happening on the other side.

Because of the general Church attitude in the Sixties we had no listening devices in the world and so were unaware of what was happening. This is true of many churches even today, and many Christians are still unaware of what is happening in the real world.

The last war brought a new dimension which had never been seen in history before. Many countries, including Great Britain, suffered the effects of war even though we were nowhere near the front line. This has always been true for the Christian. Whether a person is a 'front line worker' or whether they are in residential work they will still be under total attack of the enemy if they are seeking to do anything for God and all Christians are either active or inactive in this war.

Before invading Europe in the last war there was a massive build up of arms and supplies. The first goal of the invading boats was to set up bridgeheads in the enemy's territory. I believe the body of Christ has been on the defensive for many years and most Christian warfare teaching has been based on *defence* against the enemy rather than *on attack.* This has influenced the way that Christians have felt concerning mission, particularly locally, and it is about time that we were no longer defensive, but on the offensive. Crusades are sometimes forays into enemy territory but we need a sustained war. It is important that we build bridgeheads in enemy territory so that we can invade and claim back lives which have been snatched into his hands with little or no opposition. No war is won by defensive tactics.

An army is made up of people who have individual

skills and abilities. We have talked already of those who go out into the highways and hedges and seek to bring the message of freedom to those who are in darkness. I believe it is just as important that we build bridgeheads in the enemy's territories, to be points of contact where those who are not Christians and may not even come to Church can have some form of informal contact with those who are Christians.People have many needs; spiritual, emotional and physical. Some Christians would say that we are called to minister only spiritually and yet I believe the Bible has called us to minister to the total man.

The Devil has been using his bait for a long time, particularly through his messages of so-called freedom to hook young people and destroy them. The Christian fisherman is assisted by the Holy Spirit who is constantly out in the world seeking to reach those who are lost.

Despite the general reaction of the Church in the Sixties there were always those individuals of the body of Christ who went out and sought to reach those who were being deceived. Joan Askew, a nurse in London, took soup and sandwiches on a regular basis over a twelve year period, to Piccadilly which was the centre of drug taking in London in the late Sixties and early Seventies. There were many other individuals both here in England and around the world who were doing similar work, seeking in a practical caring way to make contact with the lost generation. Their work was thankless and they often walked in danger, but the seeds they sowed reaped a good harvest.

I was at Joan's funeral. I and another ex-addict had the privilege of being able to see Joan the week before she died of cancer. She was by then a mere six stone. We were with her when she came round and were in the privileged position of being able to feed her, whereas in the past she had fed us. She died a few days later. On her lips were the words, "Amen" (so be it).

How few know of the hours she spent talking to addicts. How few know of the care and concern that she showed to so many in various drug units, mental hospitals and prisons. How few know how many are alive today because of this one woman's faithful witness.

There have always been Christians who are in contact with the problems of the day. There are always those who are reaching out faithfully in the name of Jesus, and seeking through ministering to body and soul to lead people to the One who will ultimately transform them. Joan was one of many who was fulfilling the commission to go out into the highways and hedges. There are many alive, such as myself, because of these people who came to us in our culture and told us of the love of Jesus. There are many alive today because of Joan and others like her.

Unfortunately, when people are in this position of reaching out to those who are not socially acceptable, whether it be in prisons, clubs, pubs, or discos, the Church somehow does not seem to give them the support which many other missionaries receive in other parts of the world. The Western nations do not realise, perhaps, that they are more spiritually dark than many of the so-called uncivilized countries. The Church has not realised the need for the release of missionaries to the pubs, prisons, the clubs and the discos of our land. They need prayerfully and financially to support those with the gift of communicating with today's generation. Because of this many who are reaching out can often feel isolated and alone, and they identify more and more with the way Jesus must have felt. After all He was known as the friend of publicans and sinners and because of this was rejected by many.

Because of the attitude of the Church in the Sixties, many who were working in exposed situations, and still are, whether on the streets seeking to reach those who were lost, or whether in difficult jobs such as the prison service, probation service, or social services, or schools, etc., did not and do not receive support. Even so, they are very much light in very dark places. There needs to be a change in the attitude of the church as we need more and more missionaries to go out into the streets, pubs, clubs, discos and schools of this land and to communicate and draw alongside the generation that is being deceived. There is the need for the church to acknowledge those gifted in that way and spiritually and financially they should be released and supported to that work.

It was my privilege to spend some time with Lindsay in Cornwall. Lindsay is a British Youth for Christ worker, released under their auspices, but supported by local churches to go into schools, colleges, pubs and streets, in fact anywhere where young people are, and communicate the Gospel. This he does faithfully with the support of his wife, Marie-Claire. Others like Lindsay need support and encouragement, but there needs to be hundreds more people with this sort of ministry who are recognised by the Church and given the full respect and support of the whole body of Christ.

Bad news is everywhere, and it is time the Good News was communicated. Paul, the apostle, was a great advocate of the need to be all things to all men, and to go where they are. It seems to me that the Gospel is turned around to '*come* to our meeting', '*come* to this', '*come* to that' and yet the commission has always been to *go out*.

Many have read of Jackie Pullinger and the wonderful work that she is doing in Hong Kong. Many know of David Wilkerson and the work that he has managed to accomplish under the Lord through Teen Challenge. It is interesting to note that even President Reagan acknowledged that the work of Teen Challenge has better success rates than many government projects. The ordinary lay person anointed by the Lord has much to offer to the casualties of the permissive message.

Christine and Debbie are two missionaries in Taiwan. I met Christine sometime ago and have kept in contact ever since. She was teaching in a school in Taiwan and suddenly felt the call of God to go and reach out to some of the 80,000 addicts who are in Taiwan. God called her particularly to the prostitutes and women. At the moment she and Debbie are preparing themselves for this work with literature and are translating various testimonies into Chinese, and have been released by their missionary society for this work.

There are many throughout the world who are being called of God to reach out to those who are beyond the help of normal society. I believe we are at a point where we are seeing the Spirit of God move upon the hearts and minds of individuals in the body of Christ worldwide and I believe that God's strategy and timing is perfect. They are going into the enemy's territory and seeking to reclaim lives which Satan has claimed for his own. I emphasise that there need to be many more people who catch the vision and therefore get the support of the Church to go out with the Good News to the many who are receiving only bad news

Many in our world are coming to the point of realising that many problems are beyond the help of men. We know that where Man gives up God takes over and does a miracle. There are many like myself who through being reached by Christians and through coming into a living relationship with Jesus have been set free and now have new lives. Many of us know that *if* anyone is in Christ they do become a brand new person inside. (2 Corinthians 5:17)

Paul emphasised the need not only to proclaim the Gospel but to come alongside and meet with people. To those under the law, Paul said, "We come as one under the law". Some parts of the Christian Church have become yet another sub-culture, and like most subcultures are isolated from society as a whole and unable to communicate.

Any town of any size should have at least one or two workers released by local churches. If one church cannot raise the support and finance necessary then a group of churches could easily do so, and perhaps if the Body of Christ worked more as one there would be a greater resource both spirtually and physically to be released into the dark world that we live in.

We as Christians are the stewards of the mysteries of God. We are the ones who have the answers to the world's problems. The only problem is that the world does not know this. We need always to be seeking to bring the light of Jesus to the places of darkness. We have, however, to be sensitive to what the Holy Spirit is saying (1 John 2:26) and to be led by Him. If we go out in pure emotional response to the need of people in difficult situations, then we will quite quickly come very badly unstuck, unless our eyes are totally on the Lord and our feet rigid on His word. We have within the scriptures all that we need to be fully equipped to do any good work, (2 Timothy 3:16) and that includes setting free the addict, the sexual deviant, the emotionally bound up and the demon-possessed

Perhaps the most essential lesson to be learnt when dealing with addicts or people from other problem situations is not so much what we can do, but what we *cannot* do. We have to know what God has equipped us for and keep within those limits. We know that God can meet the total need of every individual we come across, and yet it is up to the individual as to whether they will respond to the Lord or not. The first responsibility of the Church is to make sure that they *hear* and understand the message, and we can only do this by going out to them.

We must start from the basis that we are involved in spiritual warfare and therefore can only fight with spiritual weapons. We need to be filled with the Holy Spirit, and if we are to be any good to anyone we need to go fully controlled by the Holy Spirit. If we go by emotional prompting we will soon end up shipwrecked, and many have lost both their faith in people and God through stepping out unwisely. (Galatians 6:1)

The Bible tells us to count the cost of everything we

are involved in. If anyone is thinking about and moving out to help those who are from problem backgrounds, he or she must count the cost before starting. It will be a painful, demanding, exhausting and challenging ministry. You will probably see some die or return to their old lives amongst those to whom you seek to reach out, and it can hurt when you have put many hours into their lives. You may possibly come under physical attack, lose property and be hurt emotionally. You will certainly come under spiritual attack.

Jesus knew when He came to earth that He was going to die in a very painful way, so that we may have life. We need to ask ourselves whether we are willing to suffer pain and hardship, emotionally, physically, financially and spiritually so that others may live.

Because of the life of Joan many are alive today who would have been dead. I am alive because of a young girl who came and told me about Jesus. Because of the loving and caring outreach of many Christians around the world life is being offered to many who are bound up and dying.

Despite the thinking in some circles that young people are against the claims of Jesus, there are many who are very open to the Gospel. They may not want to know about theology, men's traditions and rigid services. They do however want to know about Jesus. One good thing that has not changed is that Jesus is still the friend of publicans and sinners, and if we are friends of Jesus we need to be aware of this. Sometimes we may need first of all to come as friends and later the opportunities will come to share with them about their heavenly friend.

CHAPTER 7

Building Bridgeheads

"At the time of the banquet he sent his servant to tell those who had been invited, 'Come, for everything is now ready.'

"But they all alike began to make excuses. The first said, 'I have just bought a field, and I must go and see it. Please excuse me.'

"Another said, 'I have just bought five yoke of oxen, and I'm on my way to try them out. Please excuse me.'

"Still another said, 'I just got married, so I can't come.'

"The servant came back and reported this to his master. Then the owner of the house became angry and ordered his servant, 'Go out quickly into the streets and alleys of the town and bring in the poor, the crippled, the blind and the lame.'

" 'Sir,' the servant said, 'what you ordered has been done, but there is still room.'

"Then the master told his servant, 'Go out to the roads and country lanes and make them come in, so that my house will be full. I tell you, not one of those men who were invited will get a taste of my banquet.' "

Luke 14:17—24 NIV

During my time as a Christian I have been involved for many years with coffee bar work. I am currently involved with a Christian coffee bar run under the auspices of the YMCA. The daily work is done by individual members of the Body of Christ in our local area, and because of my travelling ministry I am very much an absent leader. Just as both prayer and finance should be released to enable individual Christian missionaries to go out into various secular situations in our society, so the local churches gathering together to finance and start coffee bar works and Day Centres are building bridgeheads in the enemy's territory. They are providing a place where people can meet with Christians in an informal setting and also providing a bridgehead from which Christians with evangelistic gifts can springboard into the various situations in society, and therefore come across the younger generation. Contact is therefore made with young people with problems. With the mixture of secular and spiritual activities young people who have never heard the Gospel can be brought into a spiritual environment, and perhaps for the first time realise that there is a God who cares for them. The coffee bars themselves are a symbol of God caring.

A 'womb' can be created into which new life can come and spiritual growth can be encouraged. I am privileged in the coffee bar to have Anita, who was on drugs for many years, helping on a day-to-day basis, and because there is a telephone there many are able to get in touch with her and she is able to share with many of her own experiences of seventeen and half years on drugs.

Recently, because of my travelling, I have realised

that there is a need for greater continuity and stability at the coffee bar and so it was decided that there should be a person who could do the day-to-day work. This was shared with prayer partners and an eighteen year old young man called John came forward. Within weeks support poured in for him to be released to develop the coffee bar work. Later Heather, another young person, came and joined the team and so God provided individuals to fulfil His work.

The coffee bar is an outward sign of the concern of local Christians in the body of Christ in a rural area for people who do not know Jesus. Much contact is made both with ordinary young people and anywhere where there are young people today one comes across the drug problem as well as emotional and spiritual problems.

It is quite surprising to see the response when a ministry becomes known as a place that cares. Many people with drug problems and parents of children on drugs either ring or write to us at the coffee bar, and many letters also flow in from prisoners and children in care. Ordinary youngsters who have not had contact with Christians come in, sometimes to play pool or on the computer, but contact is made.

We are very aware in our work that we are representatives of the Body of Christ of that area and in many ways are only reaping what others are sowing in prayer. There is a management committee made up of older people who prayerfully and practically support the work and encourage the helpers at the coffee bar in the work they are doing and seek to facilitate it.

Obviously we have to be sensible and responsible in

the work that we are doing. I fully believe that there should be a mixture of spiritual and secular activities, introducing people to the place and ministering to the soul and body so that ultimately the spirit will be affected.

It is my privilege now and then to spend some time with the Bethnal Green Mission in the East End of London. The leader is Vincent, a young married man, who with a young team of people reaches out to young people in the Bethnal Green area. Many who come in to play pool, or to take part in other activities come into contact with the Christian Gospel for the first time. Teams go out from this mission to various schools and other situations and seek to reach out in the name of Jesus. They sometimes facilitate other people in mission in their area. This again is something that is being repeated all around the world in various inner city situations, yet problems with young people are not limited to the inner city. More and more rural areas need to take up this vision and reach out to this generation.

Ideally any work like this should be supported and facilitated by the Body of Christ of that area. This is the ideal, but it does not always work out in practical terms if there is much division in the Body.

It is important to watch out for the problems that come through mixing trying to help people on drugs and seeking to reach out to young people generally. I know when I was on drugs in London the place where I knew I would be certain to buy drugs at any time on a Friday night was a Christian work in Oxford Street in the West End of London! I knew that if I went there during the night I could buy any drug that I wanted because the people who were using drugs were using that place and therefore drugs would be available for sale.

Any coffee bar ministry or day centre must provide a safe environment. Drug pushing must not be allowed to go on and people attempting to do so should be isolated from the place and dealt with on a personal basis, unless of course it is specifically a drugs help centre. We see people individually if they come with drugs problems, but through the telephone and through the letter-writing ministry, both Anita and I are able to influence and encourage many young people who are seeking advice and guidance on drugs and other problems. Many parents are also helped.

In these days of unemployment the churches have a tremendous opportunity and should respond quickly now, as there are many young people who are hanging around on the streets with nothing to do. We know that there are many and varied reasons as to why people go astray and become involved in destructive life styles, but certainly boredom and lack of vision for life can be exploited by those who have drugs to sell. I believe the young can be open to both good and bad influence. We need to make sure that the good influence is on offer!

A coffee bar or day centre can be set up relatively easily where a group of people are concerned and committed. Many look to the State or Social Services or the Police for the answers to social problems. This can relieve people of what they feel is their own personal responsibility to the youngsters with problems in their area. Cain said to God, "Am I my brother's keeper?'' and many are saying this today. Another aspect of the Welfare State which has not been good is that people feel that they have no responsibility for the problems in their area, because there is a department somewhere either in the local council or Government that will sort out any problems. The responsibility lies with the individual member of the local community, and particularly with the local church. I am convinced that coffee bars and day centres which are Christ-orientated and manned by people who are full of the Spirit and have the heart of God can have a tremendous influence and will provide life to many people who are trapped on drugs or other destructive ways of life. They can act as the centres seeking to counter the false information that is getting through to young people from the pushers and others who seek to share their ideas on life with them. The coffee bar can be a resource for parents and a place where they can find both practical and spiritual help, also a referral point for those who do want help and perhaps need the deeper help of a residential centre to come to. Usually a telephone number becomes known and a form of contact which is being explored by many Christians is the telephone counselling service, otherwise known in some areas as 'helplines'.

For many years the Samaritans in England have been well-known for being a last resort for people who in their desperate situation can ring for unbiased advice and help, day or night. This vision has been taken up by many Christians and in the South West of England there are three telephone ministries under the name of Crossline, based in Plymouth, Exeter and North Devon.

There are many other telephone counselling ministries both in this country and around the world. Advertising a telephone number and offering help is providing the caller with the opportunity of sharing without having to come face to face with a Christian, and as long as that Christian is sensitive to what the Holy Spirit is prompting them to say, and willing and able to listen, real contact can be made with those who have problems.

It is a fact that many people come to a crisis point in their lives and it is then that they are likely either to commit suicide or be trapped deeper into drugs or drink and so end up worse off, or they can turn for help *if* they know where to turn. I am impressed by the calibre of people I know who feel that what they have to offer is time and an open ear. There are many who are involved in this sort of ministry who are older and perhaps even housebound and cannot get out. They are however able to be used of God to bring hope and light to any who ring for help. By advertising a telephone number whether in the pub, club, disco, a telephone box or even the toilets, one can very quickly come into contact with people who have problems. There are many older members of the Body of Christ who have years of wisdom gained through walking with God and who have much to offer. This is one way in which they can be involved, even if it is not in meeting face to face with people who have deep problems.

I know some who have been kept alive through having someone that they could talk to confidentially, and there are many who are now Christians who through a crisis time in their lives rang a number which was available to them day or night. (They can then be referred to a physical point of contact for help.)

Stan had started on drugs through losing a leg in a motor-cycle accident. Through the years his life fell apart, and slowly but surely painkillers became the centre of his life. At a time of crisis he came across a woman called Diana. She said that he could ring her any time. As the crisis deepened in Stan's life so the phone calls came more frequently. Sometimes Stan rang in the middle of the night and yet always found Diana there ready to talk. Eventually Stan became a Christian. One of the main factors in his decision was that Diana was willing to listen to him at any time, day or night, and eventually she prayed for him and he came through to the Lord, and is now drug free. He now runs his own successful building business and is involved in reaching out to people in trouble.

There are demands that will be made upon any person who enters into this sort of ministry. There is no ministry that spares anyone from spiritual warfare and therefore attacks will come if you step out into this realm. However it is a relatively easy task to set up a counselling ministry that will bring you into contact with the younger generation. It is a pity that some feel that only older people can do a ministry like this and it would be good if some young people took on this sort of ministry, as the young can influence the young. Anyone reaching out to people will, in time, come across a common problem of 'what do you do when a person asks for *immediate* help?' The simple answer to this is that if we are in contact with people who may want immediate help we should have our lines of communication built with others who are involved in the ministry.

A picture I felt the Lord gave me once was of railway stations without railway lines in between. This seemed to illustrate that many people are doing individual works and there is need for communication between all who are involved in a similar ministry. Through Prison Fellowship we seek to provide links between those involved with prisons or in after care so that we can support and do a better job. So contact needs to be forged between all who are involved with people who might need the total scope of care of spirit, soul and body. The person who is on the telephone needs to have people (if they are not able themselves) who can provide the practical follow-up to a call. So often the resources of the Church of Jesus have been untapped because of division and people not linking together. No army could function this way and I believe that we will soon see people linking together more. Those railway lines of communication and relationships need to be built and as more people are called into this very important ministry of reaching out to those in need they need to find their own gift and link in with others. So the telephone counsellors should be backed in prayer and have at their finger tips day centres or home situations which may be open to those who ring in. There may need to be the back-up team of those who can visit people in their situation and also a place where people can go for immediate help. We should again not shun the advice and help of professional agencies even if they are secular, as not everyone may be ready to respond spiritually straight away. A homeless person may suddenly decide they want help and in this case immediate help may have to be offered. The good

Samaritan lodged the person who had been robbed in a hotel for a few days until he got over his wounds. This is of course symbolic of many young people who have been wounded and robbed by Satan and may need a place to go so that their wounds can be healed. They are the casuality departments where first contact can be made. The Good Samaritan paid for the lodgings of the man who was robbed, and finance will be needed. We need outposts in the enemy's territory so that people can have bridgeheads to move out from.

CHAPTER 8

Residential Help

In reply Jesus said: "A man was going down from Jerusalem to Jericho, when he fell into the hands of robbers. They stripped him of his clothes, beat him and went away, leaving him half-dead. A priest happened to be going down the same road, and when he saw the man, he passed by on the other side. So too, a Levite, when he came to the place and saw him, passed by on the other side. But a Samaritan, as he travelled, came where the man was; and when he saw him, he took pity on him. He went to him and bandaged his wounds, putting on oil and wine. Then he put the man on his own donkey, brought him to an inn and took care of him. The next day he took out two silver coins and gave them to the inn-keeper. 'Look after him,' he said, 'and when I return, I will reimburse you for any extra expenses you may have.'

"Which of these three do you think was a neighbour to the man who fell into the hands of robbers?"

The expert in the law replied, "The one who had mercy on him."

Jesus told him, "Go and do likewise."

Luke 10:30—37 NIV

As people pray for and reach out to the casualties of this permissive age, we will find that there will come a time when immediate residential help is needed. Most residential centres have waiting lists and because there is a gap between applying to go to a rehabilitation centre, being interviewed and eventually accepted, there is suddenly a critical period during a person's life when he or she has to be looked after and cared for. This can often mean that an individual involved at street level is the one who has to respond to the practical needs.

Some say that residential rehabilitation centres are only there because the body of Christ is not functioning properly and therefore practical needs are not being met at local levels. If a person is coming out of prison he may be going back to a place where all his friends are criminals, or even his parents, and therefore the influence in the area would be just too much for him. This can be the same with people from drugs backgrounds. Because of the tremendous pressures that do come upon a family when dealing with someone with a bad social background, there is sometimes a need for those who are specialists to provide a space for people to be able to go for long-term specialist help.

In my own work I have come across individuals in need of immediate help, but because there was no other place for them to go, my wife and I have taken them into our own home. Over the last five years we have had three people for relatively long stays. Two were directly from drugs backgrounds and were addicts, one was the wife of an addict. One of the people stayed with us for two years, another for eight months and the third person was with us for approximately four months.

We found that during the initial period of time we had to be totally committed to the people who were with us. Often this was almost a twenty four hour a day job for a short, intense critical period. Others have come for short term help. I remember talking to an old man whose relationship with his common-law wife had fallen apart and he had lost access to his child. He came to our outreach coffee bar regularly and one day it seemed right to offer him a place to stay. But this could only be on a short term basis. The area where we live is near where this man had been on drugs and he also had an alcohol problem. So I felt it important that he should be moved from this location as soon as possible. I shared this with a Christian friend of mine who himself was an ex-prisoner and he was able to offer this man a home for a few weeks while he applied to go to a rehabilitation centre.

We are in the business of offering people opportunities, although this is no guarantee that people will take them and not go back to their old ways. This man was offered the practical support that was necessary at a moment in time which was crucial to him.

The home and family is a precious resource which God can and does use as a base for much activity. But I emphasise, before taking in a Christian ex-prisoner, single parent, someone from the drugs scene or a person with other social needs, we need to pray about it and to count the possible cost of such a course of action.

Through ministering to a person's practical needs the opportunity for someone to meet with Jesus becomes much more realistic. All who are deeply entrenched in any dangerous subculture will have an immediate need to change friends and environment, and any who are seeking to help people will need the support, help and understanding of local churches and others involved in a similar ministry.

This means that Christians should not be localised in their vision, and the Body of Christ must start acting as one body. If a young man wants immediate help in an area and needs to be got out of that area, there is a need for Christians of like mind and like ministry to link together and work as one. National links need to be made. In my own prison work I very much share the vision that there is one Body of Christ ministering to the one prison system. In the same way there is one Body of Christ throughout the world ministering to social problem situations. Links need to be built between all who are ministering in this area so that the practical and spiritual resources can be shared and a more effective job done.

We have two young children and recognise that by opening up our home there is a certain risk element. But again, this is part of counting the cost, and being led of the Holy Spirit in the decisions that are made in using one's home.

It is important to be in step with God, and not just moved by emotional responses, as a time may come when your family is stretched to their limits. If there are any small cracks, these can quickly become crevasses of immense proportions.

The last thing I want to do is to put people off using their homes, but there are certain basic practical guidelines for those who open up their home for short or long-term help.

1. **Claim realistic levels of Social Security or Welfare for people who are staying with you.**

Many Christians feel guilty about asking for rent. There is money available for the support of people in your home and therefore Christians should claim a realistic amount to cover the cost of a person staying, even if they feel they do not want to claim the full amount.

You have a choice as to how you use any money that may come into your home in this way. Initially I used to claim next to nothing and found that we were going without necessities in seeking to help those in our home.

Money is available and when one considers it costs approximately £200 per week to keep an individual in prison, and untold amounts of money for people to be helped by drug units, then it is reasonable to claim a realistic amount to cover the cost of feeding and supporting a person in your home.

2. **If a person is coming to your home to get away from drink or drugs, then part of the conditions of their staying should be that they will not take drugs or go out for a drink or drugs.**

We take people into our home on the basis that they have come to *get away* from such a life. When it comes to drink and drugs starting to invade your home, then you have to draw the line.

3. **Be prepared for the fact that drugs or drink are only the surface problem of those who are coming to stay with you.**

Drugs and drink just bury the needs that are underneath in a person. There are often tremendous social, emotional and spiritual problems that surface.

4. **Be very practical concerning the telephone.**

Put a telephone lock on. Some would consider this very unspiritual, but as someone who once had to pay off a telephone bill of over £200, I advise you to think not only spiritually but practically!

5. **If someone is coming to your home, be careful that you make no long-term commitment born of an emotional response.**

I have heard some Christians say, "You can stay as long as you want, we will never ask you to leave." Later they regretted saying this and had to ask a person to leave who started to abuse their home.

6. **Do not neglect to take advice and help from people involved in the Social Service, Police and Probation.**

Local doctors can be of help as well. We had one girl in our home for two years, who had been a registered addict for thirteen years. She lived with us for two years still receiving physeptone (synthetic heroin) and we took her on this basis.

This girl has now been free of drugs for some three years and God is using her in a wonderful way with other people who are on drugs. She became a Christian, was baptised in water and the Holy Spirit, and it was only later that she actually stopped taking drugs. For her the most important part of her decision to come to our home was to leave the culture in which she had been taking drugs.

7. **Be prepared for the disruption and the lack of privacy that will come into your home.**

Weigh up the cost of this. Pray concerning whether you should make this commitment, but if you do make that commitment do not resent it during the course of the time that a person is with you, as they will soon sense the rejection.

8. **Decide before a person comes if your home will be used for short-term or long-term help.**

If you are not sure, then make it short-term as you can always change your mind and offer long-term help.

9. **Be real.**

Intolerable strain will come upon a home if a husband or wife feel they have to pretend that they always feel 'high' in the Lord, and pretend that there is never any pressure or problem. People staying in your home will soon see if you are acting out a relationship. They need to see that you are real people, that you do have times of tension and arguments, but that God is the one who helps you through. They need to see reality.

10. **Don't neglect your own family.**

The Christian home is a tremendous resource. Children can be a tremendous asset, but one has to make sure that their needs are met as well. Don't neglect your spouse either!

Fulfilment

We are talking about commitment and high cost investment without any promise of results. We are in the business of offering both practical and spiritual help, yet cannot make the decision on behalf of those with whom we come into contact.

The fulfilment of seeing a youngster walk free of problems is beyond any other fulfilment I know. It can only be compared perhaps to a young mother who looks upon a child who has been born through painful labour and is now lying upon her breast. We need, as the Bible says, to keep our eyes on Jesus, on whom our faith depends from beginning to end.

There will be pain, as there is with all physical births, there will be demands, there will be a loss of sleep and a cost in both time, emotional energy and money. I believe that it is worth it.

If you can imagine perhaps three thousand homes operating at this level — and even think of more homes opening up — we could see that thousands upon thousands of people could be helped at the critical stage of their lives, passing from the world through a home, and with support and help going out into the world changed and renewed.

I have recently come across churches who are renting flats so that if any come into their midst who do need somewhere to live they have a place available.

I believe there need to be many such places of refuge for those who need time aside to rebuild their lives.

Much of what I have been sharing can be just as applicable to residential communities. Many are doing great works for the Lord and many people are being set free through residential help. When running a house myself for three years I discovered that one could put food into a belly, clothes onto a back and provide a loving environment, and yet if someone did not respond to the Lord then the inner work was not done which would set him free from the addiction that was dominating his life.

We now have the third link in the chain. We have had the person who has gone out to make the contact, the coffee bars, helplines and other ways of making contact, the short-term help that has been offered on a local level, and now we are covering the long-term support and help that can come through a residential community where people who are specifically led of God are able to provide a loving environment. They need all the disciplines that are necessary for such a place to work, with the ultimate goal of the person walking free and able to live in the world at the end of the programme.

I am alive not only because a young woman came and told me about Jesus, not only because others came across my path and encouraged me to come to terms with my drug problem, but also because there was a long-term rehabilitation centre that was prepared to take me. Here my body and soul needs were met, in other words food and clothing was provided and somewhere to live, and ultimately my spiritual needs were also met.

There are at present very few Christian rehabilitation communities. Those that there are do a tremendous work under tremendous pressures and sometimes people who unwisely volunteer to become members of staff at these centres without weighing up the cost become shipwrecked in their faith and leave. Residential communities need a tremendous amount of prayer and financial support. Here many people are being given the opportunity to meet with Jesus and to have the initial problems in their lives sorted out. I spent seven months as a non-Christian in a community called Life for the World in the heart of England. It was there that I met with Jesus, it was there that I went through the initial working out of problems which in the past had overcome me and learnt, with God's help, how to overcome them. It was there that a loving and disciplined environment was provided to assist me as I sought to get my life together. For me, as for so many, it was a last resort. I had become desperate and at the end of myself. I think I would be quite right in saying that if the residential centre had not been there I would now be either dead or serving a long-term prison sentence.

Each part of the link in the chain is important. If there are not the residential help places available then those who are reaching out at street level or through telephone counselling ministries will find themselves with the problem of what to do with those who want to respond to get their lives together.

There are those who seem to meet God at street level and are healed miraculously straight away, but this does not seem to be the norm. Throughout the world we know of many long-term residential centres, and here in England there are a few centres ranging from Teen Challenge to Life for the World Trust, Langley House Trust, Yeldal Manor, Clouds House, and Metta House. We know that drugs and other problems relating to young people are growing larger and larger and therefore there will be the need of more houses set aside for the rehabilitation of those who have come off drugs or need a change of environment. If the Body of Christ acted as one perhaps there would be more houses available. I feel that many of the residential houses that there are, whether it be for addicts, ex-prisoners, or other young people who need residential help, do not receive the proper amount of support from the local Body of Christ that should be their due. In prison work the problem isn't people coming to the Lord but the after-care when they leave prison.

There is much pressure on Government to provide money for creating residential programmes for people with drug problems. I believe the Church has to address itself to this and other problems and ask "What can *we* do?". As with the need of support for individual missionaries in England, coffee bars and day centres, there is a need for the local Body of Christ to think about residential help places and support. Sometimes there are individuals in a congregation who feel called to running a house but cannot do it without the total financial and spiritual support of the local churches. People like this need to be identified and supported so that they in turn can be released to their ministry of hospitality and so be able to provide the initial environment in which people can come away from either the drug culture or any other culture.

It is my privilege to be able to visit various drug rehabilitation centres and houses for ex-prisoners and it is always good to go to Metta House in Bournemouth where a project funded by Bournemouth Council is led by an ex-prisoner called Derek. Many young girls from all over the country come to this centre for help with the drugs problem. There is already talk of a second and third house. It is always good to meet with many of the young girls there who have become Christians. Derek and his wife Tina are supported by Chritian staff who help in the day-to-day running of the centre and more and more support is coming from the local churches where the girls are made welcome. This is so essential for one day they are going to leave Metta House and go back into the world.

I know I was not only helped at Life for the World, the residential centre in which I found the Lord, but also helped on leaving when offered a job with the Billy Graham Organisation and given practical support on leaving there.

Some churches and fellowships may not feel led or able to cope with people who are on drugs themselves, but they may be able to supply the finances for providing a good environment for those who have come off and cannot return to the culture in which they used to take drugs, but need to go to a new place to live. Again this is an area where if the Body of Christ started to link together more concerning the problems with young people we would find much more effective follow-up. In my own ministry with Prison Fellowship we have many problems placing any brothers or sisters who have become Christians whilst in prison and who need a fresh start and a fresh environment to live in when they get out.

Residential communities often have waiting lists of people to come to them, but they also often have difficulty in placing those who are ready to go back into the world in loving Christian environments. I would encourage you to pray for all known residential centres and also to pray for many more to be raised up. It is irresponsible in some ways to start thinking about having lots of children if you have not prepared yourself for what you are going to do with them when they arrive. We, the Body of Christ, should be praying that God will provide the cradles and nurseries that will be so necesssary for those who are going to become Christians whether it be from prison, alcohol, drugs or emotionally damaged backgrounds. We should also be aware of the tremendous problems facing those running centres and daily lift up staff at such places. I am convinced there is a need for a number of open communities to which young people can go to receive help, healing and support. There are many Christian communities around the country ministering to the needs of Christians. We need *more* to specifically be geared towards young peoples' needs. Many young people are homeless and no longer have contact with anyone who cares, so often need somewhere to go for long-term support and readjustment. We need to pray that God will raise up communities able to respond to the individual needs of the young.

CHAPTER 9

Prayer — A Spiritual Weapon

In the same way, the Spirit helps us in our weakness. We do not know what we ought to pray, but the Spirit himself intercedes for us with groans that words cannot express.

Romans 8:26 NIV

And pray in the Spirit on all occasions with all kinds of prayers and requests. With this in mind, be alert and always keep on praying for all the saints.

Pray also for me, that whenever I open my mouth, words may be given me so that I will fearlessly make known the mystery of the gospel, ...

Ephesians 6:18,19 NIV

There has been a constant emphasis that we are involved in spiritual warfare. The message in the Sixties which was launched upon the young people had its origins in Satan rather than in the heart of Man. We see Satan as our enemy and know that warfare has to be waged against him. We recognise the need to be on the offensive against the strategies of Satan as well as on the defensive against his attack.

I am convinced that intercessors hold the key to much of the spiritual work that happens in our country. In the last war many people, whether Christian or not, had moments of silence and times of prayer concerning the war, particularly around the time of the imminent possible invasion of England, and also before the invasion of Europe. One of the saddest reflections on the attitude of the Church in the Sixties is that they did not seem able to see what was actually happening to the hearts of young people. There was no vision, no spiritual insight. Through all the different aspects of the message offered in the Sixties, Satan was able to enslave and destroy thousands of young people, and this continues.

In my work in Prison Fellowship I am very aware of the need for intercessors to pray and intercede in the Spirit and wage war upon the enemy. Some time ago God gave me the picture of intercessors being the artillery and the bombers which flatten the enemy opposition and prepare the way for the frontline troops. Artillery and bombers need to know what their target is and need to have reports back on the effects of the attacks. The spiritual artillery and the bombs have been falling in the wrong places for many years and many bombers have not even left base! Artillery shells and guns have remained silent or pointing inwards towards Christian-orientated activities rather than outwards to the world. Because of this Satan has managed to consolidate his hold upon the world and upon the hearts and minds of young people. Many of us believe in the imminent second coming of Jesus, however, some do not seem to realise that there will also be a manifestation of the spirit of the Anti-Christ. We are seeing things done publicly that used only to be done in private. I believe that we are heading towards a confrontation which will be seen with visible eyes between the forces of good and evil. We will see spiritual warfare enacted upon the streets as happened in the days of the Apostles. We are beginning to see something of this in the hearts and lives of many young people who have been totally bound by Satan and who have been set free and used by God for His glory. God is taking people who were 'no hopers' and giving them hope, and using them as symbols of hope to a lost generation.

Any work of God is founded in prayer, and intercessors need information and encouragement. As intercessors become more informed about all the different problems that are happening in our society and as they intercede and pray with groanings and signs, weeping for those who have been deceived, then I believe we will start to see a change. Despite the depths of depression that thinking about young people's problems can cause, there is light, and where there is the greatest darkness the light shines brightest. More and more young people are becoming Christians. More and more young people are being set free. We are seeing miracles happen.

As intercessors mobilise and pray and agree together in the Spirit, then I believe we will see Satan's hold upon the young slowly but surely shaken. I encourage all intercessors to bring before the throne of God young people in our nations. I would encourage you to pray for the young people who are ensnared on drugs and permissiveness. I would encourage you to pray for the

Christian young people who somehow would not become soldiers of the cross, but civilians. Pray for a burden to burn within them to reach their own generation.

I would encourage intercessors to be informed concerning the social issues and the different aspects of demonic influence that come into a life through drugs; be informed concerning sex abuse and incest, for it is through these experiences that we see Satan's unclean spirits and other methods, manifesting his evil work in the lives of those who suffer such abuse.

I am aware of the power of prayer. It was when I was in Pentonville prison thinking about going to the drug rehabilitation centre that one day I changed my mind. I had given a false date of release and had allowed myself a couple of days in the West End of London on drugs before going to the rehabilitation centre. A few weeks before being discharged I changed my mind for no apparent reason and got in touch with the Welfare Officer who then informed the rehab. centre that I would be coming on the date that I was getting out. I am convinced that if I had not gone on the date of discharge I would never have made it to the centre. It was only later that I discovered a group of young Baptists had been praying for me, and I attribute the change of heart to the prayers they offered up on my behalf.

I am often sad that people only consider intercessory prayer as being something that older people do. There is great power available to many young people who catch the vision of intercessory prayer and pray from the heart and the spirit.

I do believe that intercessors need to keep themselves covered. In an ordinary war if bombers and artillery are getting through to the enemy, then this will encourage a counter-attack of some sort. I am convinced that if someone intercedes, particularly for the drugs situation, they will certainly be counter-attacked by the enemy. Remember that nothing can come between you and the love of God, whether it be principalities or powers, both on this earth or in the heavens. (Romans 8:37—39).

All the different forms of help that are offered need to be undergirded and underlined in prayer. All of us who are alive today from various bad social backgrounds have been prayed for and sometimes over many years. One girl I know was prayed for for over twelve years, and as a result twelve years later became a Christian.

If you read the letters to the Churches in Revelation you will see there that all the churches were influenced by the towns they were based in. God gave them an encouragement, a rebuke, and always a way out of their situation through repentance.

I believe what we learn from this is that Christians are affected by the society around them. In the world at the moment people invest money for either a short-term profit or a long-term investment. In many ways it is the same when dealing with praying for individuals or situations which are in our society. We read in Exodus 17:8—13 the account of a battle that was directly affected by prayer. Joshua was one who fought the physical battle for which Moses, supported by Aaron and Hur, interceded. To me this indicates that there will be pain and strain and the need of support for those who are seeking to pray. So obviously the longer one prays for an individual the more painful it can become and perhaps discouragement can set in.

Just as there is the need for money to be invested in short-term profit and long-term investment, so I believe there is the same need for prayer to be directed to those two goals.

It may be that we will not see the result of our prayer for a long time, and yet we have to have the vision to know that as we pray those prayers are being channelled to the purposes for which we are offering them to God. We are reassured as particularly we pray in the Spirit that we are praying in tune with God's purposes and I believe that His purposes are to bring healing, deliverance and light to the many who are bound up and in darkness.

There may continue to be the tendency to put all the focus upon the Joshua side of the activity, in other words those who reach out and are evangelists in this day and age, but we must remember that it was Moses, Aaron and Hur in the background who won this particular battle. The battle flowed to and fro according to the position of Moses' arms.

Intercessors are indeed the artillery and the bombers. May those bombs and shells fall in the right place. May they shake the enemy and release those who are bound up in drugs and permissiveness. In the last war, preceding the landing of troops in Europe, there were artillery barrages laid down and many bombing raids were made by the Air Force in preparation for the invasion. The people of Europe were waiting to be liberated. So there is a need for the intercessors (artillery and bombers), to prepare the way for a spiritual invasion of Satan's territory.

CHAPTER 10

Prayer Applied

Jesus, once more deeply moved, came to the tomb. It was a cave with a stone laid across the entrance.

"Take away the stone," he said.

"But, Lord," said Martha, the sister of the dead man, "by this time there is a bad odour, for he has been there four days."

Then Jesus said, "Did I not tell you that if you believed, you would see the glory of God?"

So they took away the stone. Then Jesus looked up and said, "Father, I thank you that you have heard me. I knew that you always hear me, but I said this for the benefit of the people standing here, that they may believe that you sent me."

When he had said this, Jesus called in a loud voice, "Lazarus, come out!" The dead man came out, his hands and feet wrapped with strips of linen, and a cloth around his face.

Jesus said to them. "Take off the grave clothes and let him go."

John 11:38—44 NIV

I myself came from what is known, as a 'care background'. A person who has been in care is a person who either because of problems in the family, through unreasonable behaviour or through the need for protection, has been placed into the care of the local council or welfare. It is estimated that a minimum figure of one in ten suffer sexual or other forms of abuse within care homes. Some are able to cope with this sort of background quite easily and get through to lead perfectly normal happy lives. Others however find that through the childhood experiences that they have had and through feeling either rejection, bitterness, hatred or whatever, their lives have been interfered with at a vulnerable age and they never fully recover from the effects of these experiences.

I myself was diagnosed a psychopath with schizophrenic tendencies. This was the label that psychiatrists and psychologists put upon me because my background of illegitimate birth and two adoptions had affected me in such a way that I could not care less for anyone else. I had no feelings. In some ways I could understand people labelling me this way, as I then went on to spend many years in various forms of trouble.

We all react differently to the things that happen in our childhood. I am convinced that the way we are treated as children has a direct effect on the way that we will treat others as we grow up.

It was in November 1970, late at night, that I prayed, 'Jesus if you are real, come into my life'. I think for the first time in my life I felt totally accepted, forgiven and part of a family. It was later on that an important event happened in my life when I acknowledged God as my Father.

The Bible says that God is the father of the fatherless. This means that He has special concern for those who have missed out emotionally and physically in not having a family life. There may be those who have had a family life but one which has not been ideal. Many of the men and women I share with talk of bitterness and hatred towards the person who, many years before, has either rejected or hurt them. As a Christian I have come to the point where I recognise that all the bad things that have happened to me during my childhood have at last been turned towards a good use (Romans 8:28).

One of the symbols of the Holy Spirit in the Bible is oil. This symbolises healing and soothing. I know that God has healed and soothed those areas of my life which needed this. A word that people hear in Christian circles nowadays is 'emotional healing'. If you have appendicitis then you submit yourself to a surgeon who cuts you open and takes out whatever is causing you pain and will ultimately cause your death. In similar ways there are many people who have hurts which are emotional and spiritual within them which need to be dealt with. I have found that God has very gently dealt with those inner hurts both in an individual way but also through Christians who have loved and supported me. A boil can be very painful until it is lanced. An ulcer, although not seen by people on the outside can cause a lot of inner pain. So spiritually and emotionally a person could have been suffering much pain for many years.

In my work in prisons and with young people I find

most of them need specific prayer for things that have either happened in their childhood or experiences they have had when on drugs or involved with the occult. Sometimes if a person has been sexually abused I find that they need healing prayer concerning the actual incident and also deliverance from the ongoing consequences of the experience. In other words through the incident Satan can gain access to a person's spirit, so direct prayer is needed to set them free from this influence.

After coming to Jesus people usually need applied prayer and ministry. A living illustration is in John's gospel 11:43—44. Here we see Lazarus had been brought alive by the power of Jesus but needed to be set free by his friends. Jesus said, *''Take off the grave clothes and let him go''*, and I believe this is the command of Jesus to us. Many are brought to life in Jesus but many still have the grave clothes around them hindering them from walking on in new life. Perhaps this could account for so many who backslide and go back to their old lives. The responsibility lies with us who are ministering to make sure that we have done all we can to be instruments of healing and deliverance.

Often we simply need to apply the word of God to the situation that we are dealing with. There are many books on emotional healing and deliverance, and there are many who now teach on these subjects. However, there does come a time when we need to apply that which we have been taught to the situations that we are dealing with.

We are seeing many miracles happen. People with incurable diseases are being healed through the power of the name of Jesus. We live in a society where through technological advances we also have hospital facilities which minister to the physical needs of people. Over the years, because of the neglect of teaching and practising of healing in the churches, we have also seen the uprise of spiritualist churches and others who claim to have the ministry of healing.

In the Church we have both extremes of belief. Some believe that Christians should not have a cold or 'flu', or any other manifestation of sickness in their body. Others do not believe that God is interested in, or able to heal people. As always we have to search the scriptures to find a balanced answer to all the questions concerning healing. I hope in this chapter to open up the Scriptures on all the different aspects of sickness, both emotional and physical, and perhaps give an insight into how God works in this realm. Although many are healed of sickenesses, for which we praise God, there are many who go forward for healing who are in fact not healed, either at the time of prayer or even later, and sometimes die of the sickness that was prayed for. This I believe can often lead to confusion, and people have been known to go away from God because of the lack of understanding of the mind of God on this matter. God can, and does, heal both physically and emotionally, but it is not as black and white or simple as some make it out to be. I will concentrate mainly on emotional healing and deliverance as this is very relevant to today's situation.

First and foremost, as with any subject, we must start from the basis that the Bible gives all instruction for us so that we can know how to act in any given situation. (2 Timothy 3:16, Amos 3:7). We have the privilege of seeing Jesus and His life portrayed in the Bible, and seeing the way that He dealt with the situations and needs which came across His path. We also have the Old Testament to look into, from which we can learn many things. (1 Corinthians 10:1—13).

When Jesus came He demonstrated His authority over all realms: He stilled the storms, turned water into wine, multiplied the loaves and fishes, healed people's sicknesses. He cast out demons, forgave sins, raised the dead and rose from death Himself. He did all these things, not seeking to impress an audience, but as the Saviour, demonstrating with signs and works that the message He was bringing was coming with the full authority of God. He refused any glory or praise for any miracle which He performed, and often told people not to mention that it was He who had been the instrument of healing, but to glorify God for what had happened. He constantly attributed the miracles to the fact that the Father was in Him (John 14:9—11). He also promised that those who followed Him and believed in him would do even greater works (John 14:12—14).

Electricity is a great source of power and energy, but it has to be understood and handled by people who have a full knowledge of how it works, or it can bring death to those who are handling it. How much more is this so when we are handling and becoming channels of the power of the living God.

There are three main causes of sickness or afflictions and we will go through them and see what the Bible teaches:—

Cause 1: Demonic

(Matt.17:14—20. Matt; 12:22—24, Matt 9:14—29, Mark 7:25—30).

In the first reference we see a boy suffering from epilepsy. This was demon produced and dealt with as such. In the second we see that deafness and dumbness were demon caused. Again in the following reference we see a girl with an unclean spirit. There are of course other cases like these in the New Testament and this is just a selection. Most of us recognise that when we become a Christian we make a friend of God and an enemy of the Devil, and straight away are thrown into spiritual warfare. (Ephesians 6:10—20, 2 Corinthians 10:2—4). The first thing that we must realise is that Jesus was able to discern or identify the cause of the sickness, i.e. demonic, and secondly He was able to deal with the cause. Jesus spoke a word and the demon left. Jesus was in constant contact with the Father and had the full authority of God flowing through Him, and we too have been promised this authority so that we can become channels for God to use (John 14:12—14).

We can see from these scriptures that deafness, blindness and dumbness *can* be caused through the presence of a demon. However, I must hasten to say that this is not always so. Of course we still have pop music which makes inroads into the lives of many young people through the type of music and the words that are presented. I believe that as a direct result of this there are many who are under the influence of unclean spirits, as at different stages of their lives they have allowed them to come in. Many from a homosexual background need sensitive deliverance. Those who are troubled by nymphomania, that is excessive sexual desire, need sometimes to be set free from the influences of the Devil. As we step out into the world with the healing ministry and the authority that was in Jesus we need to really pray that we can have discernment.

Cause 2: Natural body weakness.
The result of the Fall.

(Mark 7:31—37, Mark 8:22—25, Matt. 9:27—30).

In the first reference we see Jesus healing a deaf mute. Here no demon activity was mentioned, and so laying on of hands became the instrument of healing. Notice also that He put His fingers into the ears and spat and touched the tongue. Again notice that in this reference Jesus charged them to tell no-one.

As we look through the passage we see that they 'besought Him,' with intercession, not just a simple request. They begged Him. Someone was concerned enough to speak to the Lord on behalf of the one in need. Perhaps we do not see much healing today because many want the miracles but don't like the blueprint of disciplined prayer and fasting which points towards a preparation for healing.

The next reference speaks of a blind man. Again, no sign of demon activity is mentioned and so Jesus uses the laying on of hands, and the spit rubbed on to the eyes. Again, the people brought the person to Jesus. Notice also the two touches. Sometimes God works this way, healing at different stages. The Holy Spirit can be compared to the wind moving in one way and another. God has no set pattern. *'His ways are not our ways, His thoughts are not our thoughts.'* (John 3:8) Again, in the last reference we see two blind men healed. They themselves had the faith to seek out Jesus. Here again He touched their eyes. Again the emphasis, or the warning, was given to tell no-one, but to glorify God.

Cause 3: Sin — Mind — Soul — Psychosomatic Illness

(2 Timothy 3:1, Hebrew 12:15).

In the first reference you see times of stress mentioned, in the second the root of bitterness

It is commonly acknowleded that some sickness can be caused through stress. Ulcers, migraine, nerves, heart trouble, and many sicknesses of the mind and body can be caused through bitterness which leads to body malfunctions.

Abuse of alcohol, drugs and even over-eating can cause many illnesses. So many diseases can be brought upon oneself through one's lifestyle, habits and attitudes. Many people addicted to drugs or alcohol have an emotional cause for their addiction. Usually when this is dealt with the addiction falls aways.

As far as the root of bitterness is concerned as mentioned in Hebrews, many suffer from joyless lives, whether they are Christian or not, because they have suffered at the hands of others, e.g. a girl could be bitter towards men because of a bad experience which happened to her in the past. Perhaps she was assaulted or jilted. With the thousands of children in care in England alone, there are many who have suffered at the hands of those who were supposed to be caring for them in their childhood. This becomes part of their personality and make-up, and they in turn can have an attitude of hate or bitterness towards all authority.

Although the pornographic industry is very much to blame for the amount of sexual assaults and other perversions that are prevalent in our society today, it is interesting to note that many who become homosexual, whether male or female, have had some sort of incident in their younger years which has been the lever towards them becoming involved in their type of lifestyle. Many young men I have talked to who have committed sexual offences against children were themselves offended against at an early age. Of course there are always exceptions to the rule, but as you become more involved in this area of society you find that those facts surface more and more as you share and minister to people. Because of the number of marriage break-ups and the weird situations that one comes across today, i.e. incest, both partners living with separate partners in the same house as the children from the original marriage, adultery, etc., many are affected at a young age and a warp in their personality develops as a result. Even after a person becomes a Christian the full flow of the Holy Spirit through a life can be hindered through past experiences which are not resolved.

Some perhaps can be bitter because others have got married whilst they remain unmarried. Perhaps they are fat, short, tall, thin, wear glasses, etc. The Devil can use these things to hinder them and cause them to stumble if they are dissatisfied with God because of the way they are. They are precious in His sight and He will meet their needs while here on earth, and if they have to get through life missing out on something, He will reward them accordingly when they get to heaven. (1 Corinthians 2:9—11) Are they divorced and feel bitter, or perhaps widowed? God is especially close to them as well. (Psalm 68:6) Are they suffering from physical disability? They will one day have a new body. (Phil.3:21).

When we come to Jesus we become new people (2 Corinthians 5:15—21). As we forgive others then we will experience a release in our own life (James 5:13—18). Because of our past, and even our present experiences, we can be of service and help to other people, or we can hug our sorrows and be bitter about how hard done by we are, and so end up imprisoned in our bitterness. I do not pretend that it is easy. I feel especially sorry for those young girls who have ended up becoming single parents and suddenly have all the emotional pressure of having to bring up a child on their own. God is close to them, and God can and will help them, not only to cope with their situation, but also to be of benefit to others. (2 Corinthians 1:3—7). As we in turn receive ministry, so then we can become channels of ministry to others.

We have to learn to lead people into forgiving others for wrongs they have done to them, and towards receiving the forgiveness and deliverance of God in the areas which have come under the domination of the enemy. We need to pray over the things in the past which can affect the present. This is a demanding ministry where those who are seeking to minister need to keep very close to God, and be very sensitive as they are led by the Holy Spirit to bring deliverance and peace to those in need.

In this day and age, even though we have advanced medical science, we still have many diseases that are caused by modern living e.g. teeth come out through eating too much sweet food; much food contains chemicals through the fertilisers that are used to force growth; more and more food is impregnated with preservatives and flavouring which can affect some people in their behaviour e.g. hyperactivity. There has been more information circulated lately concerning additives in food and some do react in a violent way. We have a whole new realm of mental sickness and mental hospitals overflowing, so much so that many patients are just doped up so that they will sit around all day and not cause any problems. This is mainly through under-staffing and the lack of resources to minister healing to so many who are in need. Many are treating sicknesses of the soul or spirit with medicine only. A living experience of Jesus can and does indeed heal. There is always a fine line, and too many times people try to have hard lines as to what the Bible teaches. If someone is in contact daily with the living Saviour, this can lead, and indeed often does, to the refreshment of the body and total healing of the mind. (Proverbs 3:5—8). I believe there are certain requirements for healing:—

1. Discernment: Matt. 4:23,25.

We see in this scripture that many people came to Jesus and He dealt with them individually. He knew if the sickness was demon-caused or not. Sometimes

He led people to the forgiveness of sin, sometimes not. We must allow God to guide us to what the actual need is. We also need to know whether we need to fast and pray, and whether we ourselves are going to be the instrument of any deliverance or emotional healing.

2. Be known for our lives: Many people were either brought to Jesus or came to Jesus for healing. It was the same with the Apostles. They were known to have the power of God with them. People will come to us if our lives inspire faith in God, also, if God knows that He can trust us to minister to any He might send along.

3. Faith: We see that there was always someone who had the faith to believe for healing. In the case of the paralytic who was lowered through the roof we see that Jesus saw 'their faith' (Luke 5:20). Sometimes the person themselves had the faith to believe. Faith is the key.

4. Love: Love can be a great healing force. It can restore people and bring them to wholeness. It is essential to see people as individuals and restore to them their dignity and self worth.

Developing a relationship with someone and inviting them into your home can have a healing effect on life. To become the father to the fatherless, mother to the motherless, brother or sister to the person who needs this sort of relationship, all these are important as this can bring healing to a whole range of emotional and psychological sicknesses, being a rock to the weak so that they can tie on to you for a time until they can be restored. However this aspect of ministry makes great demands.

5. Having the mind of Christ: 1 Corinthians 2:10—16.

We must see people as Jesus saw people; lost and hopeless, having His compassion and forthrightness, recognising that only in Jesus can we meet any needs. We must know our own weakness. (2 Corinthians 3:4—6) and we must realise that only the Spirit can bring the healing power of God to people who need to know this ministry in their lives.

6. Authority: We must appropriate the authority we have in Jesus to bring freedom and deliverance to those who need it. (Matt. 18:.18—20).

Two-pronged Healing Ministry

To the non-Christian: Mark 16:17—18, Matt. 10:1, Mark 6:7—13, Luke 9:1.

In these scriptures, and also all through Acts we see the ministry of healing to the world. Too often healing is confined to a big meeting or totally within church-held meetings. We must realise that we have the authority, if so led of the Lord, to deal with people at this level as we come across their path. We are ambassadors for Christ. (2 Corinthians 5:2—10). So any born-again believer, whether ten years old or fifty years old can be used as an instrument for God in this realm if we are open to this. Nearly all of the healing of Jesus and the Apostles took place outside the Temple, and was not organised. They met the needs of people as they came across them. Perhaps this is something we can think and pray about. The disciples at the time of Jesus were bickering etc., yet God still used them. So we too must realise that God can and indeed will use us if we make ourselves available and move when He tells us.

Healing confirmed the gospel. Currently much of the gospel is preached in church when it is supposed to be preached to those who do not know it. Perhaps this is the reason why signs and wonders do not precede or follow the gospel as they did in the early Church. The commission was to go out into all the world and preach the gospel. Then the scriptures go on to say, these signs will follow. The individual born-again Christian, led of the Spirit, must begin to realise the potential within to minister healing and deliverance to those who come across his or her path. We are meant to be the Body of Christ in this world. When people were brought to Jesus things did happen. People were healed and delivered. It was never intended that becoming a Christian was to be a totally academic experience of just learning the Bible and becoming a local church member. Each person who comes to know Christ has the potential of becoming an instrument for God in a very powerful way.

To the Christian: James 5:13—18.

There is obviously a ministry also within the Body of Christ. However, perhaps many healings do not take place because there is so much unconfessed sin in the Body of Christ, gossip, envy, strife, position seeking etc. Perhaps people are so used to looking to men for their teaching and guidance that somehow they have not been pointed totally to the Lord who will supply all their needs. Remember that God wants to move through the individual members of the Body of Christ. In this passage we see that oil is mentioned, and this is a symbol of the Holy Spirit, indicating healing and soothing. There are many who need to be healed and soothed in body and mind. However, I believe that much ministry and counselling would not need to take place if people had at least one or two friends or brothers in Christ with whom they were totally open and secure in their friendship. Confession is part of the historic gospel which many Free Church people have somehow thrown out as being not of God. This is a great pity as we all need to confess our sins one to another, perhaps not in the confessional sense of the word, but in an open sharing relationship where there are those to whom we can go and be open with about the things we have done wrong, and receive disciplining and counselling. As God heals within the Body of Christ we must give Him alone credit. People need to be like Jesus and keep things quiet if someone is healed, or at least keep quiet about the instrument used, but praise God and testify to what Jesus has done in their body.

Healing of the mind is also a Church ministry and when a person becomes a Christian there is often much healing and restoration to take place in a life, so that the young Christian can come to a mature walk with Jesus.

I believe we need to be free to minister to one another, rather than waiting for the leaders or teachers who are better known to come around. I believe that God wants to move through His body, so that we in turn can minister healing, deliverance and faith to each other and then to the world.

A person may still choose to go back to their old life but we must be at peace in so far as we have done all that is possible for them. Sometimes prayer needs to be accompanied by either those involved or those supporting fasting. It is important I believe for the Church to identify those with a prayer ministry and set them apart for counselling and ministry. Sometimes I feel too much emphasis is placed on teaching gifts and not enough on this aspect of ministry, to the detriment of those who are in need. Prayer is the foundation we move out from and through intercessory prayer war is fought on behalf of those who are in the enemy's clutches. It is through applied prayer that people are set free to walk in new life. Each is important and just as intercessors need to keep their guard up, so those praying personally with people need to be aware of the cost of ministry. Often through seeking to bring healing and deliverance we can find ourselves under much attack and going through problems such as face those we are reaching out to. Jesus was called the friend of publicans and sinners and in the same way suffered rejection similar to those who are publicans and sinners. As He suffered and was tempted so we will be, but as we carry on reaching out we will find ourselves in a God-given and true priestly role (Hebrews 4:14—16).

CHAPTER 11

Equipping in the Holy Spirit

Finally, be strong in the Lord and in his mighty power. Put on the full armour of God so that you can take your stand against the devil's schemes. For our struggle is not against flesh and blood, but against the rulers, against the authorities, against the powers of this dark world and against the spiritual forces of evil in the heavenly realms. Therefore put on the full armour of God, so that when the day of evil comes, you may be able to stand your ground, and after you have done everything, to stand.

Ephesians 6:10—13 NIV

So far we have considered prayer applied in emotional healing and deliverance, and now we examine the fundamental base we move from. We need to be equipped spiritually to do spiritual works. We need spiritual weapons to fight spiritual warfare.

I hope most Christians would agree we are living in the days of real spiritual warfare. I believe we are living in the days when the Devil is like a roaring lion seeking to devour (1 Peter 5:8). I think it would be a mikstake for those living in Western Nations to feel that they are better off than the Christians being persecuted physically throughout the world. It is very hard for us sometimes to recognise the warfare that we are involved in. Many Christians are backsliding, and I believe the Devil has had a real victory in that Christians in the Western Nations have become largely impotent in the face of the onslaught of permissiveness and violence that pervades our society. I believe part of the reason for so many who are struggling and not being used to their full potential is the lack of understanding of the role and the power of the Holy Spirit in their lives. Many debate the issue of the Baptism of the Spirit, the second blessing, or other such ways of describing this experience. There is enough scriptural foundation for the experience and being baptised in the Holy Spirit and speaking in tongues was for me not just an optional extra but a necessity to be able to get free from a destructive lifestyle. I am aware that there are those who have had this experience and are still not effective spiritually or have gone back to their old lives but this doesn't disprove this experience of God. There will always be those who misuse God's gifts. Besides being filled with the Holy Spirit we also need to be aware of the diversity of gifts and how to apply them to the situations we are in.

I think it is important to understand that:

1. **God calls and equips.** The people often felt weak and inadequate (1 Corinthians 1:26—31).
2. **It is possible to lose the anointing of the Holy Spirit** and to be disciplined by God. However, there is always a way back to God and that is

through genuine repentance. (1 John 1:6—10, Hebrews 2:1—2, Hosea 5:14 – 6:35).

3. **Suffering goes hand in hand with being led of the Spirit** (Hebrews 13:12—14, Hebrews 2:14—18, Hebrews 11:23—40).

4. **People were anointed not only for 'spiritual tasks' but also for very practical purposes** (Exodus 31:3—6, Colossians 3:23—24).

We recognise that God the Holy Spirit was at work in the Old Testament. We have already touched on the prophecy of Joel, which foretells the coming of the Holy Spirit in a wider way than was ever seen in the Old Testament (Joel 2:28—29), and another scripture which follows on from this, promising an individual relationship which was not had by everyone in the Old Testament (Jeremiah 31:31—34). In the Old Testament we see God the Holy Spirit moving upon individuals calling and equipping them for the tasks that were laid before them. I believe the baptism of the Holy Spirit is given to us so that we may be witnesses (Acts 1:8), that we may learn to hear God for ourselves personally (1 John 2:26—27), and that we may be fully equipped in the world.

Jesus came to die for all that we have done wrong, to die in our place so that as we personally receive and commit our lives to Christ we might be set free from the punishment of sin, and also the burden of sin as we live our lives in accordance with God's rules. Before His crucifixion Jesus shared many deep truths concerning the Holy Spirit. He also promised that we would do greater works than even He did. (John 14:12—17). He underlined this later in John's gospel (John 16:1—15).

There is much emphasis placed on the fruit of the Spirit (Galatians 5:16—24) and of course this is very important, and yet the love of Christ was proved in the way that He set people free from the influence of the Devil. He was totally submitted to the Father, so the Holy Spirit moved totally through Him.

I believe God wants to move through His body in the same way as he did in the Acts of the Apostles, through individuals like you and me. Some would say that the Baptism of the Holy Spirit was just for the Apostolic days and yet we see Pentecost referred to as a fulfilment of prophecy for the last days (Acts 2:17). If Pentecost was referred to as the last days, how much more are these the last days that we are living in. Some are confused through seeing people who claim to be baptised in the Holy Spirit and indeed have been baptised in the Holy Spirit go astray and sin openly or misuse the gifts that have been given to them. Obviously many do this after knowing Jesus, but we do not reject Jesus because of the way that some people behave claiming to be Christians. The Bible does say that the gifts and call of God are irrevocable (Romans 11:29). In other words, yes, there are people who misuse, abuse and glorify the gifts rather than the giver. They will be judged for this before the judgement seat of Christ. However, we must look to ourselves and to all that is contained in the scriptures concerning the gifts. We are told that God does not want us to be uninformed and we are encouraged to earnestly desire to prophecy and not to forbid speaking in tongues (1 Corinthians 12:1, 1 Corinthians 14:1—40).

Remember, to resist the Holy Spirit is to resist Jesus and the Father. They are one. We must therefore be open to what God wants to give us for we need all the help we can get to be fully equipped for the spiritual warfare in which we are involved (Ephesians 6:10—20).

When we receive Jesus we receive the uniform of the army of God, and when we receive the Spirit in all His fullness, we receive the potential of all the weapons of our spiritual warfare. Those weapons are for waging spiritual warfare in the world, not necessarily that we become perfected in corporately singing in tongues or dancing in the Spirit, important though this might be, but that we may rejoice in seeing captives set free and new souls coming to Christ as we step out in ministry into the suffering world. I believe some of the lessons to be learnt from the New Testament are:—

1. **God is not tied to any formula.** Some were baptised in the Spirit with the laying on of hands, others had the Holy Spirit come upon them, and so it is today. God's ways are not our ways and His thoughts are not our thoughts. Each person is treated individually.

2. **There are six specific promises concerning the Baptism of the Spirit.** (Matt. 3:11, Mark 1:8, Luke 3:16, Luke 11:13, John 1:33, and Acts 1:5). It is mentioned more than the term 'born-again', so commonly used in this day and age.

3. **We are told to seek and to ask for the Holy Spirit and his gifts.** (Luke 11:9—13, 1 Corinthians 14:1,39).

4. **Linked with the Baptism of the Holy Spirit are often scriptures referring to refining.** Sometimes after the initial blessing can come a time of God showing things in our lives which are bad and need to be dealt with. The symbol of the Holy Spirit mentioned there is fire and fire refines metal by burning out the dross. There is also a time of testing and training in spiritual warfare. (Matt. 3:11,12, Luke 3:16,17).

5. **God is not mocked.** We are warned not to treat this gift lightly and judgement is promised for those who do (Hebrews 6:4—8, 2 Peter 2.20—22).

6. **We are told to lay hands on no man hastily.** People must be prepared for the Baptism in the Holy Spirit and warned of the consequences of misusing any gifts that are imparted. Sometimes past occult experiences have to be dealt with first, also bitterness or the need for emotional healing before a person can freely receive the fullness of the Spirit (1 Timothy 5:22, Matt. 18:18—20, Hebrews 12:12—17).

7. **Everyone's experience of the Baptism in the Holy Spirit is different.** Some can be very joyful, some quiet, some manifest the speaking in tongues or prophecy on being baptised in the Spirit, others do

not. This however has no reflection on whether a person is or is not baptised in the Holy Spirit (Luke 11:13).

8. **The baptism in the Spirit is separate from conversion.** (John 20:22, Acts 2:1—4, Acts 19:1—6, Acts 9:14—17).

The Baptism in the Holy Spirit is a scriptural experience. One would need to make a deeper study to fully understand the manifestation of the gifts of the Holy Spirit both corporately and in the every day witness to the non-Christian. Love should be the basis of all that we are involved in (1 Corinthians 13). We must resist the Devil (James 4:7) and be constantly filled with the Spirit (Ephesians 5:18). In fact we are told to go on being filled and not to grieve the Holy Spirit in our lives. We will realise both through the Old and New Testament that being filled with the Holy Spirit can often mean a part of suffering and rejection as this is what happened to Jesus. No baby is born without some pain being suffered and therefore as part of the preparation of being used by the Holy Spirit we might find ourselves going through times of testing and trials, yet as we go through these we will realise how weak we are and how strong God is. I believe God's burden is that we should be as Christ was on this earth to those with whom we come into contact, and we can become the instruments of deliverance and healing to those in our world that have need of this ministry. As always there are cautions and guidelines how we should minister in this realm, and we need to stay very close to God and very aware of our weakness if we are to be used in any ongoing way. The word baptised comes from a word which basically means to be immersed. Just a water brings life to a desert, so the living water that is within us can flow out to the world and bring life where there is death. We need to learn from what happened to many in the Old Testament who were touched by God and yet went their own way and eventually ended up away from God. We need to be encouraged as we see God moving in the New Testament through men of weakness and yet men who were channels for the power of the Holy Spirit. God will never force His gifts upon anyone. This includes of course the precious gift of Jesus the Saviour of the world. It also includes the gift of the Holy Spirit in all His fullness. May God fill us with a thirst for the Holy Spirit that we may indeed know what it is to have rivers of living water flowing from within us. (John 7:37,38, Rev. 22:17). May the Holy Spirit give us sensitivity and an awareness of other people's needs and the authority to minister God's healing, deliverance and wholeness in a world that is devoid of real love. May we introduce people to this third person of the Holy Trinity who wants to set people free from their pasts and help them to live victoriously in the present, equipped to go back to others who are still bound up.

CHAPTER 12

The Christian Response to Permissiveness

''Come now, let us reason together'' says the Lord.
Though your sins are like scarlet, they shall be as white as snow;
though they are red as crimson, they shall be like wool.
If you are willing and obedient, you will eat the best from the land;
but if you resist and rebel, you will be devoured by the sword.
for the mouth of the Lord has spoken.''

Isaiah 1:18—20 NIV

Christians today are having to face a world geared more and more to sex and perversion. Some are beginning either to succumb to the temptations that come with the lowering of Christian standards of behaviour or are doing the opposite by turning their back on the world and refusing to face the problems that exist. In doing this they are perhaps at a loss as to what to do when faced with a person in need.

As always there is a middle line. Christians are called to be salt in the society in which they live. It is hard to be a chimney sweep without some of the dirt brushing off on you. It is just as hard to be involved in the world without being affected by its influences. However, the Bible gives us all the teaching we need to know what to do in any given situation (2 Timothy 3:16).

There is a real need for healthy teaching on sex and sexual behaviour and relationships. Instead of being avoided it should be taught in an open and clear way by the Church. Films, records, plays, TV and books often present a picture which is totally unrealistic in its approach to sex. The media also distorts what relationships are all about.

For the unmarried this can be very difficult. Many young men and women learn to masturbate at an early age. This can lead to a life-long habit, with the accompanying deep guilt feelings. After a person becomes a Christian there are usually areas in the sexual realm which need to be dealt with. Books and advertising titillate the senses and in most cities, unless you go around with your eyes closed, it is hard to avoid seeing things that are sexually stimulating. Obviously, some people have more of a problem in this realm than others. Some would say that men have more problems on the whole than women. With men it is often the pressure of physical desire which causes them to stumble. With women it is the emotional need which can lead to sexual problems, as many young women end up in sexual relationships through the desire to be loved and accepted and to overcome feelings of rejection.

In our churches we are having to deal with people who are the direct products of the permissive society in which we live, so we need to have a healthy and biblical approach to any to whom we are seeking to minister. We need to be sure where we stand ourselves concerning our attitudes towards those who are mixed up in society's various perversions and what sort of bibilical help we can positively offer them when they ask questions concerning Christianity and the application of the Bible to sexual problems.

Homosexuality: (Leviticus 18:22, 20:13, Genesis 19:1—29, Judges 19:16—30).

We need to have some sort of understanding of why people who are homosexuals have been involved in this realm. Obviously in saying this I mean both men and women, as the problem is rampant in both sexes.

One cannot be a practising homosexual without denying the Christian faith. We are living in the days when we hear of gay churches, gay weddings, gay vicars and church leaders. There are those who would say that it is quite consistent to be a Christian while still being a practising homosexual. This is, of course, wrong and it is a sin. However, God does love the homosexual and God wants to meet his or her deepest needs. This does not alter the fact that sin is sin, no matter which way we look at it. If someone steals, that is sin; if someone commits adultery, that is sin; if someone is angry or condemns, that too is sin. We have to see homosexuality in the context of sin and at the same time not see it as any worse than any other sins prevalent in our society today. (1 Corinthians 5:9—13).

When talking to homosexuals I tell them that according to the Scriptures it is just as wrong for people to commit adultery and to sleep around as it is for someone to be a homosexual. This brings things back into context. God can and indeed does heal and deliver from this way of life, and many have found a true deliverance in the Lord Jesus. The Christian working in this situation needs a great amount of understanding, discernment and a loving firmness.

When trying to find the cause of becoming a homosexual one soon realises that there can be a thousand and one reasons. Sometimes it can be a sexual experience which happened when they were much younger. For instance, a lesbian that I know became one through a rape experience when she was fifteen years old. Maybe the way some dress or look has encouraged homosexual advances. Some move into the homosexual way of life at first for mercenary motives and later become hooked on that lifestyle. Others become bored with normal sex. As there are many different causes so there are many different ways to minister.

My personal belief is that homosexuality has come about, as have many other sexual deviances, as a direct result of our permissive society. The scriptures do tell us that when truth is suppressed and when people do not honour God they become futile in their thinking and their minds become darkened. An almost direct result of this is idolatry or worship of images of either creatures or men, and also sexual impurity leading on towards homosexuality as the end product. (Romans

1:18—20).

Many young people become trapped through their involvement with pop music. It is interesting to note that more and more pop groups are becoming bisexual in their looks or blatantly homosexual or bisexual in the images they project to the young people. This does make an impression on eight or nine year olds who watch and are involved in the music of these groups. Now we also have the video industry which is also a cause of many sexual problems in our society.

It is very hard for young people sometimes to escape the trap that is set before them. As the laws of the country are changed and as some are directly opposed to the laws of God there will always be conflict of opinion. However, those who are listening to what God is saying will remain faithful to His word and the Holy Spirit's prompting. A scripture I keep emphasising is 2 Timothy 3:16. In this scripture we see that within the pages of the Bible are all the answers to all the questions. We can be fully equipped with the Holy Spirit if we look deeply for the answers.

The killer disease 'AIDS' is rampant amongst homosexuals causing a lot of fear among the 'gay' community. It is acknowledged that this disease will become more and more widespread and even if the cure is found I would not be surprised if other diseases relating to homosexuality will surface. You see, God knows what is best for our bodies, and when He warns us about what is right or wrong, there are reasons. There are always physical and emotional consequences in the lives of those who go against God's laws.

Permissiveness: (2 Peter 2:1—22).

As with the homosexual scene, we find that sex outside marriage is accepted as normal. Again this is encouraged through the media. Girls or boys who openly say they will wait until married before they will have sex are condemned as weak and silly and become a target for fun and cruel jokes. To those who say that there is nothing wrong with sleeping around or with a permissive society, one has only to point to the consequences which are seen within our own society here in England, i.e. children in care, abortions, the divorce rate and also of course sex-related diseases which come through a promiscuous lifestyle.

It is sometimes hard for people to understand that God warns us, not because He is a spoil-sport who wants to stop any pleasure or fun, but basically because He created us and knows how best we will be fulfilled. It would be crazy to do the opposite to what the makers instruct with our latest washing machine, car, or hi-fi, and yet this is what people do with their lives. God has given us our bodies and laws so that we can get the best from them and protect ourselves from incurring the results of sin in our body.

We have to be sensitive and firm when dealing with people who have come from this sort of background. Bad habits don't go away overnight, and sometimes many will have great battles trying to lead a normal life after being involved in some of the sexual situations we have in our society today.

Some will need deliverance and healing in areas of their lives. Girls will feel impure, and have to be taught that God accepts them as clean, because once they repent and turn to Him for forgiveness they are as virgins in His sight.

Men have to do battle, and I know that I myself found it very hard to come to terms with not sleeping around after becoming a Christian. It was not something which disappeared overnight, but God gives the strength to be able to cope, because God loves us and God understands us. The message we have is always the same; sin is sin. We can be forgiven and God will help us to overcome. He is always there to help us if we fall. We need an honest and open relationship with Him as He continues to love, support, and help us. As Christians we need to have this same attitude towards those to whom we are seeking to minister.

It is God's plan that we should enjoy all His gifts, including sex. We have only to read the Song of Solomon to see the romance and pleasure that there is to be had between two who are totally committed to each other. This helps us to realise that God indeed has a great undertanding of the gift He gave us. Eve was given to Adam as his help-mate and the two became one flesh, totally unified (Genesis 2:24). However, you can see in Genesis that the first effect of the Fall was that they became aware of their sex organs, and were ashamed and tried to cover themselves (Genesis 2:25 and 3:7). All through the Bible we see sex and God's attitude towards the uses and abuses very plainly set out. In the judgment of Sodom and Gomorrah we see God's attitude towards permissive cities. (Genesis 18:16 and 19:29). In the New Testament we are warned of the ultimate result of permissiveness in our society (Romans 1).

Sometimes people fail because they do not understand basic scriptural principles and therefore come unstuck with every spiritual battle that comes across their path. Many Christians blame Satan but most of the time people are their own worst enemies, because they have a lack of understanding of themselves. With sex and relationships we must have an understanding of the fact that we are a three-part being; body, soul and spirit. Part of us cannot be involved in anything without it affecting the other parts. (1 Thessalonians 5:23—24, Hebrews 4:12). We need to communicate this.

The Body: It is easy to understand the physical aspect of ourselves; physical desires, the need for food and drink, sex, natural desires, seeing, hearing, touching, smelling, tasting, feeling.

The Soul: The seat of emotions ("I feel"), our wills ("I will/won't"), our minds, intellect, thoughts ("I think/I don't think"). We often hear of 'Soul music' and music can affect the soul and affect us emotionally.

The Spirit: That which is born again of God. (John 3:16). When we ask Jesus into our lives we are born again. In some ways, asking Jesus into our lives is like conception, and most of us know that there is a long way between conception and an adult walking around the earth. So, when we are born again we are born with all the potential of adult spiritual life. As we receive from God in the spirit, so this affects our soul, mind, intellect and will. This in turn should affect our body the things we do and say, etc. So the order is that we receive through, and by, the spirit from God. He comes and dwells in our lives, giving peace and so working out His will through our spirits, souls, and bodies.

How does this affect the sex realm?

Physical love: i.e. be sexually attracted to someone and sexually involved with someone. Some people form a relationship and marry only at this level.

Love from the soul: i.e. be attracted by not just the physical, but by the personality of a person. Again, a lot of people marry at this level. This leads to a relationship which is based not just on sex, but on enjoying the same things, emotionally and physically.

Love in the spirit: i.e. if you are a Christian the Lord leads you to someone. You love them and are drawn together in the spirit. The spiritual relationship has already been formed through Christ, leading on to an emotional soul, love relationship, and ending up in completion physically through marriage.

Therefore, a Christian can love in the fuller sense. That is the order in 1 Thessalonians 5 — Spirit, Soul and Body. The Lord draws you by the Spirit. This leads to the Soul, and may then lead into the full relationship of marriage. You come totally together in all realms. In the world it can so often be physical first, and if a person is not a Christian, next the soul and then marriage.

God has guaranteed to supply *all* needs (Philippians

4:19). He knows what is best. It is sometimes easier to trust God for heaven than it is in many other realms. Now that I have children, I sometimes find that I have to restrict them from doing certain things, for example, playing near the fire or on the road. They can become very angry at these restrictions, but I am doing it for their own protection because I love them. Later, of course, they will understand this. They will realise that what held so much appeal for them could have hurt them badly or killed them. As they grow up, they will also understand that, because I love them I didn't want them hurt. So it is in our relationship with God. (Isaiah 55:8,9). God knows what is best for us, especially where relationships are concerned. If a person trusts Him for salvation, then they can trust Him also to provide the partner for life (if this should be the life plan). God knows every one intimately (Psalm 139:13—16). So He knows exactly what people need. In Genesis 6:2 we see that people chose who they wanted to marry and we can see the result. Be warned, because this is a decision best left to God. *He does know what is best,* and will lead you to a person if you are to be married. Be patient. He knows when you will be ready to marry. He is already training your partner.

Why am I saying these things?

I know that this is an area of life which people have difficulty in understanding. They are physically attracted to a person and for some time they have a good brother/sister relationship in Christ. They go out with each other and it all folds up. Sometimes this is because the carnal nature comes up, or maybe they have entered into a deeper relationship than the Lord intended. Often they can never again reach the same depth of relationship after this. They cannot reach the same area of trust and sharing again because of upsets. How often do we hear "The Lord led us together" yet within a few weeks it is all over with embarrassment all round? So often too we see Christian men or women go out with non-Christians, and then see the results in a ship-wrecked faith. Let the Bible be our instruction book. (Joshua 23:12—13, 1 Kings 11:1—8, 1 Corinthians 6:14—18). The Scriptures are quite plain as to the wishes of God. And remember, God is thinking of our ultimate good.

Obviously the sex realm is one which affects some people more than others. some will have come from a very promiscuous lifestyle and find it very hard, as I did, to readjust to a life which is based on Christ, and His guidelines. Others might live in a fantasy world, dreaming of what it would be like if they'd had a chance to have a life as a non-Christian before they became a Christian, and the Devil can build on this.

Like all wonderful gifts from God, the Devil seeks to pollute and cause misunderstanding of not only the gift, but the giver. So we must really stay close to God in everything that we do in our lives. God wants people to live free of bondage and condemnation, and to have fulfilled relationships. Remember, Jesus Himself was never married, so He must have suffered many of the pressures that those who are single suffer. He does understand (Hebrews 4:12—16). As we seek to communicate these truths we will be true representatives of Jesus.

Other people may be apparently having a good time. Most of my friends were married by the time I was twenty. When I saw them ten years later, many of them were no longer together. Most of those who were still married were struggling with a weird sort of love/hate relationship. Some of the girls who slept around had babies to look after. Many of these had been left to cope on their own. Never condemn anyone who has problems in this area. You could be in the same situation but for the grace of God. Don't be like a Pharisee, but be like Jesus, firm, compassionate and understanding.

Some look to sex as a release from the pressures of life. Others seek for love and affection which they have not received from their parents or others (Romans 2:1, 15:1, Galatians 6:1—5). The scriptures give us advice on how to help those who are struggling. Take refuge in our Lord at all times.

We need to have a positive approach to this whole subject and to come across as people who are motivated by love from within rather than as condemning and pharisaical in our attitude and outlook. We need to take a firm and open stand against those who are seeking to use the sexual vehicle to make money and to enslave people and to stand up against any religious leaders who purport to be of the Christian faith and condone immorality. However, there is also a time, as with the adulteress at the well, when we need to seek to minister the love and forgiveness that can be found in Jesus Christ our Lord. (John 3:17).

CHAPTER 13

Practical Guidelines

Therefore, my dear brothers, stand firm. Let nothing move you. Always give yourselves fully to the work of the Lord, because you know that your labour in the Lord is not in vain. 1 Corinthians 15:58 NIV

Be on your guard; stand firm in the faith; be men of courage; be strong. Do everything in love.
1 Corinthians 16:13,14 NIV

Brothers, if someone is caught in a sin, you who are spiritual should restore him gently. But watch yourself, or you also may be tempted. Carry each other's burdens, and in this way you will fulfil the law of Christ. If anyone thinks he is something when he is nothing, he deceives himself. Each one should test his own action. Then he can take pride in himself, without comparing himself to somebody else, for each one should carry his own load. Galatians 6:1—5 NIV

If anyone has caused grief, he has not so much grieved me as he has grieved all of you, to some extent — not to put it too severely. The punishment inflicted on him

by the majority is sufficient for him. Now instead, you ought to forgive and comfort him, so that he will not be overwhelmed by excessive sorrow. I urge you therefore to reaffirm your love for him.

2 Corinthians 2:5—8 NIV

In recent years some have come to know the saving grace of our Lord Jesus Christ whilst serving prison sentences and have gone on to be ordained or become leading figures within the Body of Christ. Today many more are receiving new life in Jesus Christ whilst serving prison sentences and are seeking to serve the Lord during their sentences and upon discharge. Sadly, some of these are falling by the wayside after release and are returning to crime and sin. The reasons for this are many and varied but Christians outside the prison walls must accept some of the responsibility for this.

Many members of the Body of Christ are asking what mistakes are being made and a growing number of churches are asking how they can be more effective. Such questions indicate that members of the Body of Christ want to learn to be effective for Christ in helping to reach out to and help ex-prisoners come to Christian maturity.

In my own life I know the importance of people first of all coming to me where I was and secondly giving me both practical and spiritual support needed initially to find Christ and eventually to grow away from the lifestyle that was killing me.

Just as there seems to be a new move of the Spirit concerning in our prisons in England and worldwide so there seems also to be a new awareness of many of the social problems which are afflicting the young today. Because of this I felt that I should give realistic guidance and advice to help those who could be termed the casualties of the permissive age that we live in.

Some aspects of this advice may appear to be harsh and uncompromising but it is born out of the experience of those in the front line. Men and women have suffered deep anguish following mistakes at the expense of those they have been trying to assist. Their desire to share some of these costly mistakes brings hope that your caring may be more effective. The advice is born out of the scars of people who have gone before. The Word of God is a living gospel which is as relevant today as it ever was. It is through the Word and the prompting of the Holy Spirit that brothers and sisters in Christ released from destructive ways of life will be led to maturity in Jesus. Take the words of 1 Corinthians 3:1—2 into your heart, and lead brethren lovingly and firmly into the Kingdom. The enormous help of many Christians in compiling this advice is greatly valued.

We are now in a position in England and Wales where many from social-needs backgrounds are accepting Jesus Christ as Lord and Saviour. This gives us good reason to praise the Lord, but we need to think on to the next stage, that is, what happens after they come to know the Lord and how we can assist them in their new life. Can we help them come to spiritual maturity and what special areas of discernment and understanding should we have?

First we need to remember that we have to apply spiritual principles to all of life. We must remember the basic principle that God can meet all the needs of the people with whom we are dealing. We are the instruments of God and need to hear what God is saying both through Scripture and through the promptings of the Holy Spirit. He guides us in giving positive help to those who come across our path. (1 John 2:26). Any help that we give must be based firmly on Scripture. In 2 Timothy 3:16 we read that we can be fully equipped and that all the answers are in the Bible for any given situation. We see both in Romans 15:4 and 1 Corinthians 10:6—13 that we can learn from the situations that have occurred in the Bible. In James 3:2 it tells us that we all make mistakes and Ephesians 5:10 implores us to learn what pleases the Lord.

It is so important that we learn from one another's mistakes. I hope to convey some of this learning so that you will avoid certain pitfalls. However in making mistakes with some people, we are involved with lives which are already damaged. It is our task to be discerning and mature in assisting healing and growth and not to add to any past damage through ignorance. Ours is to learn at *our* expense, not at the expense of those less able. Let us also remember that we cannot assist anyone to do anything that he or she does not want to do or become what they do not want to be.

Giving Testimonies

It is becoming very much the 'in' thing in this day and age for people to be giving testimonies. We all have a burden to reach out to people, and there is always the danger that if a person is an ex-drug addict who has been on drugs many years we feel that their testimony would really witness to those who are still on drugs. Even though the thinking sounds right sometimes the effect can be counterproductive if the person who has shared their testimony ends up back in the lifestyle which they testified they had come from.

I felt it important to tackle this issue head-on as I am very concerned that so many I have known from my own background ended up either dead on drugs or back in prison and never managed to function spiritually.

There are many ways that premature exposure or testimony giving can be damaging, first to the person and secondly to the local Body of Christ. One mistake is to expose or allow people with sensational testimonies to be given too much publicity too quickly. It is not unknown for a person to be giving their testimony in half a dozen churches, appearing on local radio, and perhaps even becoming a youth leader or counsellor in a church within weeks or months after conversion.

Sometimes this happens through a person wanting to have platforms on which to speak. We should always encourage churches, if they do get such a person, to tell them to go back to their own people and witness to *them.* Many have suffered the pain of estrangement, loneliness and rejection throughout their lives. The act of giving public testimony *too soon* can put a young Christian in a situation they are often ill-equipped to cope with and the results can be personally damaging. The person giving a testimony suddenly finds they are accepted, embraced, held up and even revered. The inability to cope with such expressions of praise can be as unhelpful as the former rejection. Alternatively they may find such acclaim so uplifting that because of their immaturity the person is led to pursuing an ongoing ego trip which is unreal and ultimately destructive.

Sometimes it is the fault of the group or church to which the person has turned. There is always the danger of holding people up as trophies of grace, either to justify a ministry to people in need or to try to prove that Jesus is alive. If a person is pushing themself forward they need to be protected from themselves.

Children, including spiritual children, often want to take on more than they can handle and after coming to know Jesus a person needs time to put their ordinary everyday life together again (Hebrews 5:12—14).

Finding out Information

It must be understood that life within a subculture of any sort is not a normal life situation. The real tests occur after conversion when choice returns and the person is attacked with the full force of worldly temptations. It must be the function of churches and organisations who want to assist someone who turns up saying he or she is a Christian to find out more information about him or her. There are many reasons why we should do this. Firstly, if a person is in genuine need we can enquire what the real problems are, and so try to help and protect him or her from sin and of course protect the Fellowship. Many who come to Christ from drug or prison backgrounds may have never set foot inside a church before. Many find themselves in a dilemma at their first Christian contact. They are quite rightly instructed by Christians to seek out a church and spiritual home. Once outside their own environment such people will not be brimming over with confidence. Many will have difficulty in making contact with new faces and extreme difficulty in walking into a strange church where they are unknown, especially on the first Sunday after conversion or contact. Liaison with prison chaplains, drug rehabs, or other interested parties poses an immense challenge to church fellowships to be sensitive to such people on release from drugs, prison or a permissive lifestyle. It is essential that they are lovingly led to a church fellowship where they will feel comfortable and accepted as soon as possible after conversion. Much of the responsibility for this must rest with the first Christian contact but they can only refer people when Christians outside are willing to act as a link between the world and the churches.

Imagine a man turning up in your Fellowship. He tells you he is a Christian and needs support. He says he is just out of prison. On telephoning the chaplain of the prison you might find that he is in fact a con-man who is working his way around the churches, conning unsuspecting Christians for what he can get and then moving on. This does not mean that straight away you abandon him, but it does give you a chance to say, "Look, we know what you have done. We will accept you, but if you get up to any tricks here I'm afraid you will not be able to continue in fellowship with us." Such a person will then know where he stands and this will either help him to grow in attitude and not to live in a fantasy world, or he will be offended and move on.

An opportunity for repentance must always be given.

Bad situations arise too because Christians have not been given the information available to help them deal with such situations. All referrals must be dealt with confidentially and limited to mature spiritual people. In order to protect a person from the rejections of bias, prejudice, ignorance and simple damaging gossip one cannot overemphasise the need for complete confidentiality. All Christians do not have a natural sympathy towards men who are ex-addicts, ex-prisoners or from certain socially deprived backgrounds. Any information given must be treated as privileged and used with great care and discernment and always for the protection of the individual and the church assisting him.

If some Christians have a glass of wine with a meal they should be careful not to do this with an ex-alcoholic at their table as this might lead him or her back into drink or cause embarrassment. If a person has committed sex offences against children then he must not be allowed to babysit. The person who has had previous convictions for deception and fraud must only be introduced to risk with extra forethought and not given responsibility for large amounts of money or easy access to credit/bank cards or cheque books. Commonsense and Christian care often go hand in hand.

Problems arise in a church fellowship because there is generally a lack of openness. I believe the ideal is that all Christians know each other's weaknesses so that they can in turn look out for each other, but the reality is often far from the ideal. So there will come difficulties in knowing how one allows information for the protection of both the individual and the Fellowship itself to be circulated in such a way that a person can be protected from themselves, but at the same time not judged or condemned. This very much depends upon how open the church or fellowship is and what their attitude is towards what is considered socially unacceptable behaviour.

Financial Help

A person may be unable to place any real value on money and seem unable to discipline himself concerning its use. Christians need to be firm in their guidance and not provide more money than is sensible, remaining supportive and helpful and allow the person to learn lessons from their own mistakes.

Where there is a need for financial help, this must be given wisely and discerningly. Should someone need to put a deposit on a flat the church may need to respond to such a need when it is genuine. Practical support is often needed and should be forthcoming to those in need.

Always ask for advice or help

Many Christians meet failure through lack of discernment and experience in dealing with people and sometimes this is through ignorance or an unwillingness to take the advice of those experienced in this sort of ministry. It is also possible to become cynical and in such cases turning back to the scriptures may help. The key is 1 Corinthians 13 where it says *'Love believes all things'*. The need is to come afresh to those who come across our paths and try not to be influenced by what has happened in the past. The need is to learn from our mistakes, remaining open and loving and thereby more effective to those who need care and help.

Together, not in isolation

Whatever the individual ministry given to a person in need it should not be done in isolation. Confer with other Christians involved with similar ministries adjusting your own ministry as and when necessary. Where more than one person is involved with an individual it is essential that those Christians assisting speak with one voice. Children grow into stable mature adults through consistent loving parenting. The ''parenting'' must be consistent and we must not allow emotional immaturity to 'divide and rule'. Children can be experts at using subtle forms of emotional blackmail with parents to get their own way. Often a person may appear to be physically mature but emotionally they may only be a child. They may use similar forms of blackmail and Christians must be on their guard against this, making it clear that such behaviour is unacceptable.

Aspects of ministry

We may be involved in simple befriending, inviting a person to a meal on a Sunday. We may find ourselves as a family, relating to the family of the person we are helping. Whilst large lively churches can be helpful, it is often the individual relationship with one or two committed people that bring a person through to maturity. It may also be that we use Bible study and teaching, or assist a man or woman to learn to read and write, or provide voluntary or paid work. Many are unemployed and this will help to alleviate boredom. We may use the healing ministry. To have someone who will listen to all the hurts and hatreds of the past is very healing and many do need to talk and pray through such bitterness about their past and hatreds which remain unresolved. However, in seeking to minister at this level we must be aware of our own limitations in time and energy. There is also a need to help young Christians who have nothing to do during the weekdays when there are no fellowship meetings. However, the person who is demanding everything, time and money, not only in the beginning but continues in demanding time, money and fellowship at all hours and on a continual basis over a long period, needs particular direction and pointing to the Lord, as only He can supply all these needs.

Institutionalisation

Where a person has been in prison for many years or perhaps in other institutions for most of childhood, they can be emotionally damaged. Hear from one who spent many years in prison:

"I know when I personally became a Christian at twenty five years of age, I was emotionally about sixteen or seventeen, mainly because of institutionalisation and drug addiction and being in institutions all my life. I had never formed any real relationships and never had any real responsibility."

One must understand that lifestyles do affect people in a particular way. Where people have been deprived for many years of "real" choice it can be very difficult to start thinking for themselves.

A good illustration of this is something else said by the same young Christian:

"I never realised that people had to pay electricity bills, telephone bills, and it never really clicked that people cook their meals and had to pay for food."

I know that this sounds very odd, but what I am talking about is the general everyday things of life which people presume everyone knows. What can happen is that Christians can feel very hurt or confused and feel that they are being used, and yet a person from an institutionalised background is not meaning to do this. This can lead to confusion as a young Christian can be 'on fire for God' and yet find it hard to cope with the practicalities of ordinary life.

I want to emphasise that it is important to be sensitive to the struggles that people do have coming from difficult backgrounds. However, there does come a time where a person can no longer use the past as an excuse for present bad behaviour. This does mean that the Church has got to learn to enact loving discipline, which leads either to a person recognising what they are doing is wrong or alternatively going back to their old life.

In Matthew 18:15—17 we see some instructions how to deal with situations where open sin is happening. The Church as a body may need to bring discipline upon a person, but there may still be those individuals who feel God wants them to maintain contact in some form.

It is very difficult when dealing with people who might go back to death if we have to discipline them. This can cause tremendous emotional stress upon those who have to enact discipline. When I had to ask people to leave my home I found that I would be up and sick all night through the worry and tension of it. There are dangers that people use these scriptures to bring discipline where loving concern should be shown. We have to be very sensitive before God concerning how we enact these scriptures in individuals' lives. However, we must recognise that it is important to differentiate between the need for spiritual or cultural change. Remember that often people come from a totally different cultural background. Problems can be caused through Christians trying to bring about cultural changes in a person which have nothing to do with the necessary spiritual change.

A Christian ex-prisoner or ex-addict can sometimes behave in very terrible ways, perhaps sexually or by sliding back into a one-off crime or an affair. Yet often there is very little real difference between them and someone from a 'normal' social background. While their behaviour is either against the law or is clearly morally wrong, others are gossiping or going away from God in a less obvious way and without correction. Be careful how you judge the actions of any person.

In a variety of situations that I have come across I have found that much of what I learnt in teaching sessions and Bible Studies seemed to be quite irrelevant to the actual situation that I was facing. Sometimes one can go to college to learn woodwork, or the building trade and then suddenly find that even though the basis of what is learned is very good much of it is irrelevant when working on a building site or in real life situations. I do feel sometimes this is the same for many who have had teaching for years and yet have never had to apply their teaching to the real life situations that one comes across in the social situations in our society.

We do need to step out into these areas of need and accept that risk is often involved. Perhaps one of the most important things for us to understand is that people are not our enemies. We only have one enemy and that is Satan. It is Satan who is working in people's lives and who uses people to get at us. We need constantly to be aware of the satanic elements that are at work in individuals who have been hurt or damaged.

Some churches have been confused and surprised by a new believer who questions an authoritative speaker, because they do not agree with or perhaps cannot understand what he has said. This can be a form of rebellion, but sometimes it can be a genuine seeking to know the truth for himself. Many do go through a critical phase which may last for a long period where they criticise everything. In dealing with situations of rebellion, one can perhaps agree with much of the criticisms and the danger is protecting things that need not be protected. On the other hand sometimes the reaction is extreme and such a person needs to be loved and understood as they seek to find their own place in a strange and new world. With such people Christians must be patient, firm, understanding, but most of all *honest.* Remember we are like the womb in which the young Christian is growing and must expect to be stretched and bear with the birth pains as they grow up into Jesus. Often they can have a black and white attitude towards people and issues. Coming from a world of crime, utter corruption and hypocrisy they can sometimes see all too clearly the very subtle corruption and hypocrisy amongst the church and the Christians with whom they are involved. Because they often come as complete outsiders to a set of new circumstances they can indeed see a lot of wrong things. We have to be open to whatever God might want to bring to us through such people and not be threatened by what is said, and yet be firm, kind, and discerning. Sometimes it will be seen that a professing Christian is bent on self-destruction and is going back to his old ways. There does come a time to draw apart and, however sadly, allow this to happen (Hosea 5:15, — 6:3).

Concluding comments

This advice has been offered to help in situations that you may face. It is incomplete, as every situation and every individual is different. I may however have sparked off your own thinking and helped you with answers to meet your situation.

Remember that most Christians from damaged backgrounds have been helped by very ordinary people. Some believe that only people from those backgrounds can understand and realistically help. This is not true, nor is it true that 'professional' help is always the best.

In your ministry with the casualties of the permissive age His Word will become a *living Gospel.* In taking up the cross of Jesus Christ and meeting the challenge of His Word you too will grow into Christian maturity along with the person that you are assisting. The Holy Spirit will provide all your needs. It is a journey of excitement and adventure and one to be fully shared. In Jesus and in the Word of God, guided by the Holy Spirit, are to be found all the answers to all the situations that you will come across (1 Corinthians 15:58, 1 Corinthians 16:13).

In 2 Kings 7:3—11 we see four men who had leprosy. In many ways they can be compared to the social lepers of our society — the prisoners, drugs addicts, those with AIDS, homosexuals, and others caught up with the permissive life style of today. We see the city which could be compared with society or the Church locked up and under siege from the enemy.

It is interesting to see how these four lepers became the source of life to the city. Verse 9 in the New International Version reads *"then they said to each other, 'We are not doing right. This is a day of good news and we are keeping it to ourselves. If we wait until daylight, punishment will overtake us. Let us go at once and report this to the royal palace."* This indicates to me that those who are the social lepers of our society are the potential life lines for both the Church and also for society as a whole.

As God transforms, renews and sends out those from bad social backgrounds then hope is brought to many who are trapped in similar lifestyles.

Instead of a domino effect for wrong we have a domino effect for right. I was first of all reached by a young girl and a variety of other people who constantly over a three year period told me about Jesus and offered practical support. I was then supported and helped in a rehabilitation centre and ultimately led on to the resources that were available to me through finding Jesus, being taught from the Word of God, being baptised in the Holy Spirit and given power to come to terms with my past. The rehabilitation centre was the womb in which I stretched, kicked and grew until such time as I was ready to go out into the world. I believe all places whether homes, rehabilitation centres, coffee bars, even relationships are wombs in which many grow and will eventually go out into the world.

When people truly repent of their past and ask Jesus to come into their lives, then they are born of the Holy Spirit and have the Holy Spirit living in their lives. It is up to those who are helping to lead people on towards the One who will set them free and help them to come to terms with those things in their lives which are damaging them. Our goal must be like that of John the Baptist when he said *'He must become greater; I must become less'*. John 3:30 NIV.

CHAPTER 14

A Declaration of War

...For though we live in the world, we do not wage war as the world does. The weapons we fight with are not the weapons of the world. On the contrary, they have divine power to demolish strongholds. We demolish arguments and every pretention that sets itself up against the knowledge of God, and we take captive every thought to make it obedient to Christ.

2 Corinthians 10:3—5 NIV

In Great Britain on one Sunday in November each year we have Remembrance Day. All young people and children are reminded by seeing the emblem of the poppy that there were those who laid down their lives and died that we may have freedom.

We remember the wars, particularly the last war, and other wars that have been fought.

In countries throughout the world remembrance services are held and often two minutes silence observed as people reflect on loved ones they have lost or the sacrifice that was made by others on their behalf. Men and women are remembered for their sacrifice and courage.

It was in 1938 that Chamberlain returned from Berlin with a bit of paper. He thought that by having the signature upon that paper there would be no war. Those who had insight realised that war had already started and were preparing for it.

Later war was declared and people went to fight an enemy who, in promising freedom to the countries he had invaded, was inflicting destruction and death upon all who opposed him.

People in the Western democracies and other countries in the world went to war against this enemy.

Hitler deceived his nation by promising them much material wealth and freedom and a new world, and yet led them to the brink of destruction.

It is sad today that many people, particularly young people, do not appreciate what was done for us in the last war. It is even sadder that people do not appreciate what was done by Jesus who died on the cross. He showed us in his time on earth that we did have an enemy, Satan, and He laid down His life to win the war.

There came a time when war was declared upon Germany and through the nations uniting together and pooling their resources and arms, victory in the end was won. This was not without cost in both men and money.

The war would never have been won if a defensive strategy had been used all the time. There was a time for defence, and here in England we remember the Battle of Britain. There was, however, a time of attack and it would have been useless if all the arms and men that were assembled to invade Europe had remained in the camps and not passed over into the enemy's territory and started to possess the land there. The war was taken into the very heartland of the nation we had declared war on.

As Christians we need to go on the offensive against the enemy who for many years has had his way in the world. We are fighting an enemy that is seeking to destroy, confuse and kill, and has been doing so for a long time.

When Germany was eventually defeated it was found that there were concentration camps where atrocities had been committed and many were horrifed. As we come against the enemy we will find that there are many horrors that will come across our sight. We will have to look on those things that we would rather look away from, but we are called as Christians to do so. America had a choice as to whether they should fight. In the end they joined in. Most spiritual warfare teaching that I have heard concentrates on putting on the whole armour of God (Ephesians 6:10) and sometimes the impression is given that one then continues with the sword of the Spirit to fight off Satan for the rest of one's life. I am sure when the Roman soldier put on his armour that was the beginning of him entering into war.

We need to have teaching on attack, on strategy, on building bridgeheads, on invasion plans to go and take the war into the enemy's territory.

The Christian church has in many places become yet another sub-culture, rather like any sub-culture, where people have become totally isolated from the real world.

In wartime everyone is involved in the war effort. The farmer ploughing the field, the women working in the munitions factories, the people building the aircraft, tanks and making guns, are just as important as the front-line soldier. The whole nation is involved in the war effort and the whole nation's freedom is in the balance.

In many ways I feel this is the same spiritually. I recognise that not everyone will be called to go out into the highways and hedges in a physical way. However, everyone must think offensively against Satan and act spiritually against Satan, and I believe then we will see him releasing the hold he has on many people's lives.

It is reassuring for us to know that when Satan was kicked out of Heaven only one third of the angels went down with him. They were to become the demons, the agents of Satan. This means that two thirds of the angels outnumber Satan's demons two to one, which should give us much encouragement!

I call upon the Body of Christ to declare open spiritual warfare upon the enemy that has snatched away so many young lives through the last twenty or thirty years. It was when Russia, America, England and other great powers worked as one that the enemy was defeated in the last war.

As the Body of Christ recognises that it is one (Ephesians 4) and starts to work together as one, yoked in the Spirit, fighting a common enemy that we will start to see the strongholds of Satan beaten. Jesus said the gates of Hell shall not prevail against the Church. It is a long time since the Church started to try to batter down those gates.

Elisha could see beyond the physical circumstances surrounding him to the chariots of fire in the hills. The servant couild only see the physical army. We need to have spiritual vision to be able to see. The attack had come because Elisha was active (2 Kings 6:8—16). Attacks will come our way if we are active. There is no war without pain and hurt, and I believe the day is coming when Christians will no longer be always looking for blessing and for a sort of spiritual utopia in which to live in this world before they go on to the next, but will start to realise that to be a Christian is to follow in the path of Christ, which has many thorns.

When the war was eventually won there was great jubilation in Trafalgar Square and throughout all the cities and towns of both occupied and unoccupied countries. The Bible tells us that God is the father of the fatherless, *'a bruised reed He will not break, a smouldering wick he will not quench'* (Isaiah 42:3).

Once a person said to me "Isn't it wonderful that you take the news of Jesus to so many who are in the prisons and to the problem situations in our country?" My reply was that I really did not take a message that wasn't already going before me. You see, Jesus is out there already. The Holy Spirit is seeking to woo and to draw people unto Jesus so that they may know salvation. Jesus is still the friend of publicans and sinners. What has been missing has been the people out there alongside the Holy Spirit, co-working with Him to reach people.

Those who were soldiers knew fear in their lives. A good soldier had fear and he learnt to live with it and control it. God knows that we will have fear in our lives. This is why there are so many scriptures relating to fear in the Bible. As we go forward with God and seek to reach out into the world and to free people from the enemy who is enslaving and destroying them, then we will know a tremendous joy of seeing others being set free.

It is good to have a Remembrance Day, to have two minutes of silence to reflect on what has happened in the past. It may be good perhaps to have a two minutes reflection on what is happening to young people today.

The poppy reminds us of people who were willing to lay down their lives that we may have freedom. The cross reminds us of somebody who was willing to lay down His life so that the whole world may know true freedom. The cross challenges us to lay down our lives and to give of our time and money for us to spend time in prayer so that others may live.

I am alive today because someone came into enemy territory, and others both then and now released me to a new life through financial, emotional and spritual support. There are many who are waiting to be rescued and have not the resources within themselves to do anything about their circumstances.

I again challenge you to pray for the young people in our Western nations whether they be ensnared in drugs, permissiveness, the occult, or the many other temptations which are thrust across their path by a secular society that has no longer got spiritual sight. I believe Western civilisations need to throw themselves on their knees before God as they come to the brink of destruction.

So many say 'peace, peace,' when there is no peace. With all the resources that we have at our fingertips in this age, the power to blow up the world at the push of a button, the governments of this nation are bankrupt as they have no ability to meet the deepest need of their people.

In the world we see governments at last waking up to the fact that there is a massive problem with young people and much political pressure is being put on for a social action to take place. May the Holy Spirit place a burden upon the Church to go out to the many who are being ensnared and may God raise up many, many people who will be equipped with discernment, gifts of healing, deliverance, hospitality, teaching, that they may respond to the needs of the casualties of the war that we are in. Remember Jesus said — *'I live not to condemn the world as it is already condemned but to save the world'* (John 3:17).

Not all are called to be front-line troops, not all are called to run residential centres or even help in coffee bars. All are however called to be offensive in their strategy against the enemy and to work as one with other Christians.

Elisha saw the events around him in a totally different way from the servant. He had vision which was spiritual.

As we declare war upon the enemy, as we work as one, as we seek to free those who are enslaved by a cruel enemy we will see battles won, but not without cost to ourselves.

The challenge of that cross to us as individuals is, are we willing in whatever way possible to lay down our lives that others may live?

Also available from Tony Ralls

Books
Escape to Reality: £1.95
Tony's life story

Snatched from the Flames: £1.95
The story of Anita Hydes, written by Tony Ralls

What everyone should know about drugs: £1.00
A handbook for young people and those in ministry

Records/cassette
'Life' by Tony Ralls LP or cassette: £3.50

'Bitter Harvest' songs on the message of the book: £4.95 cassette. Available Autumn '87.

'Social issues — a biblical response' double cassette: £4.00 (Sides 1—3 Bible teaching. Side 4 Testimony and message)

'History of drugs/practical insights' Cassette: £2.00

Video (VHS only)
Documentary, interviews, teaching, singing. By donation to ministry.

Books and 'Bitter Harvest' cassette available from booksellers, or by post (plus 10% postage) from YMCA, Mill Street, Sidmouth, Devon EX10 0DW. Other items from YMCA only.

Proceeds from sales are channelled into the outreach ministry.